Come Follow Me

Study Book

Second International Edition, 2017

Tim Green

Acknowledgements

I warmly thank everyone who helped with this project through their encouragement, critique and prayers. Sue devoted hundreds of hours of careful scrutiny in the earlier stages of the first edition, Jacob and Rachel gave untiring help in its latter stages, and Jen was closely involved in the second edition. Michael did a magnificent job with the line drawings and David with the cover picture. Around forty believers representing the target readership in several countries kindly helped with field-testing and gave insightful comments. They must remain nameless but I am grateful in particular to S, D and J. The translators and editors of the German, Farsi and Arabic editions gave helpful suggestions. A big thanks too to my family and especially my wife Rachel. Together over many years we have shared the joys and heartbreak of those who walk a difficult path of discipleship in hostile surroundings.

Explaining this second international edition

This second international edition (2017) is very similar to the first edition (2013), with the same question numbers and page numbers. However, I corrected typing errors, simplified some complex phrases and added study tips at the end of some lessons. I made small improvements in the text of pages iv, 3(question 8), 24(q.11), 44(q.15), 68 & 76(practical tasks), 98(q.15,17) and 151(intro).

I originally wrote this course for believers of a particular religious background living in their homeland, but now there are users in many countries including the West. The worldview issues are still relevant but course leaders should adapt the discussion questions to the context.

This is the international English edition. I have used international English spelling whenever allowed under British English. This international edition is available worldwide through the website (come-follow-me.org), which also gives information about the different language translations. A separate UK edition will be published later.

Any profits from the sale of the course are used to maintain and extend this project.

Please send me your suggestions for further improvement in future editions.

Tim Green, September 2017   comefollowmecourse@gmail.com

For more information

and to download the Advisor Guide, go to come-follow-me.org.

Copyright

First published in the United Kingdom in 2013 through Lulu.com. All rights reserved. Second edition, 2017. Copyright © Tim Green 2013.

Readers are welcome to photocopy up to two lessons of this study book, or print the taster lessons from the website, in unlimited quantities but not for sale. Please do not copy more than two lessons. Or contact me at comefollowmecourse@gmail.com for further permissions.

All scripture quotations, unless otherwise indicated, are taken from the *Holy Bible*, New International Version®, NIV®. Copyright ©1973, 1978, 1984, 2011 by Biblica, Inc.™ Used by permission of Zondervan. All rights reserved worldwide www.zondervan.com. The "NIV" and "New International Version" are trademarks registered in the United States Patent and Trademark Office by Biblica, Inc.™ Scripture quotations marked NLT are taken from the *Holy Bible*, New Living Translation, copyright © 1996, 2004, 2007 by Tyndale House Foundation. Used by permission of Tyndale House Publishers, Inc., Carol Stream, Illinois 60188. All rights reserved.

ISBN 978-0-244-92809-4   Cover design by David Vosburg. www.zagmediaarts.com

Dedicated to those who strive to build a new life in Christ
and to find their place in his community,
while still caring for their families and old community
despite misunderstanding and rejection.

Please Read This First!

The *Come Follow Me* course is to help you grow strong in Christ and in his community.

This study book is not the whole course! It is only the first of three parts. So please follow this method:
- First, complete the self-study questions for one lesson (page vi says how to do this);
- Then, discuss that lesson with your advisor or in a group;
- Then, put the 'Practical Task' into practice.

These steps combine together to inform your mind, change your heart and equip your hands for practical service.

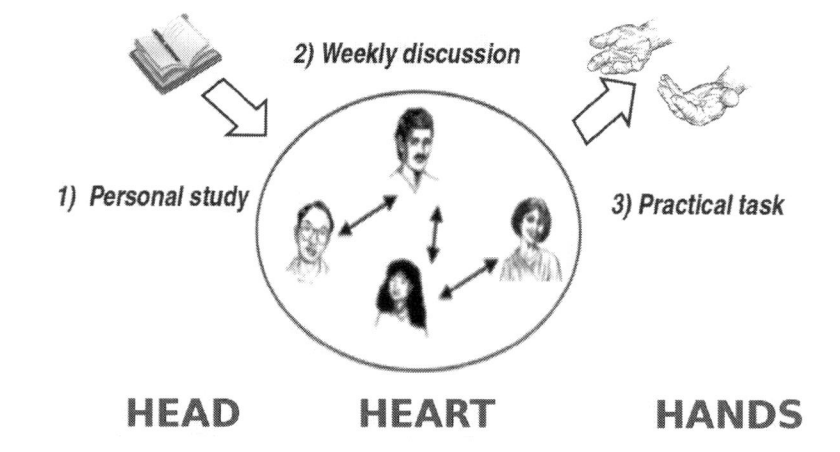

1) Personal study — 2) Weekly discussion — 3) Practical task

HEAD   HEART   HANDS

So please don't just study this book on your own. Instead, find a wise follower of Christ to help you as advisor. After each lesson's personal study, meet up with your advisor. Discuss together what you are learning and how to put it into practice. Ask advice from that person about issues in your life. Pray together and strengthen each other in Christ. You will gain even more benefit if you do it in a group with other believers.

If you are an advisor using *Come Follow Me*, please obtain the Advisor's Guide which explains how to use the course. The 'cultural clues' will help you understand the topics and there are detailed discussion questions for each lesson. Download the updated Advisor's Guide free from **come-follow-me.org** or follow links from there to purchase a hardcopy.

Whether you are a learner or an advisor, please send me your comments. Give me suggestions for improvement and tell me if you would like to know about other similar courses.

Thank you!   Tim Green   comefollowmecourse@gmail.com

come-follow-me.org

Contents

Lesson		Page
	Guidelines for the Learner	vi
1	Becoming Christ's Follower	1
2	New Life in Christ	8
3	God the Father	15
4	Obeying Christ by the Power of his Spirit	21
5	Talking with God	28
6	God's Word for Us	35
7	Members of Christ's Church	42
8	Members of Two Communities	49
9	Reasons for Persecution	56
10	Reacting to Persecution	63
11	Husbands and Wives	70
12	Solving our Disputes	78
13	Giving Witness	87
14	Baptism	95
15	The Straight Path	102
16	The Law of Love	109
17	Fasting and Giving	116
18	Fate and Magic	124
19	Serving One Another	132
20	Our Pilgrimage to Heaven	140
Supplement 1	My Daily Time with God	149
Supplement 2	How to Reach God	151
	Feedback	154

Guidelines for the Learner

1 *Welcome to this Course!* It will help you follow the Lord Jesus Christ in your daily life. I am your teacher and here are a few guidelines to help you benefit from this course.

2 Don't study this course just on your own- you will gain little benefit. Please find a wise follower of Christ to help you as advisor. After each week's home study, meet to discuss it with your advisor - and preferably with fellow-learners too.

3 And, most importantly, put these lessons into practice in your daily life! Each lesson has a 'Practical Task' for you to do in the coming week.

1. Read each question carefully.

2. Write or tick [✓] your response in the blank spaces provided.

3. After writing your response, you may check with the answers at the end of the lesson.

4. After completing each lesson, do the Lesson Review to revise the key points.

5. Some questions ask you to bring your own opinion to the discussion time. Make sure you answer these questions and be ready for discussion.

6. For the first five lessons the only text book you need is this course book. From lesson 6, you will also need your own copy of the Holy Bible. In this course, we are mostly using the New International Version (2011 edition), but if you have another translation that is fine. There are many translations of the Bible, but they come from the same text in the original languages. The original is unchanged.

7. Around the world there are many followers of Jesus Christ who come from the same former religion as yourself. Some of them are highly educated and some are not. This course is written in a simple way so that even people with less education can understand it. You may find the teaching style quite simple, but will you obey it in your life? God cares more about your obedience than your intelligence. If you obey the teaching you will benefit.

8. Remember, your advisor is giving their own time to help you. Show your respect for that person by arriving on time for each discussion time, and by completing the homework.

Now begin, with the Lord's help!

Lesson 1   <u>Becoming Christ's Follower</u>

The Purpose of our Lives

Two men were having a discussion. One of them said, "I believe that God Almighty created me to obey his commands. He sent the prophets to show me the Straight Path. If I follow that path then hopefully God will forgive my sins and let me into paradise. That is the purpose of my life."

The other man replied, "I too want to obey God's commands. But I am not afraid he will send me to the hell-fire. He has already forgiven my sins and has promised to welcome me in heaven. So, on this earth I am glad to know him personally, feel his love and love him too. I want to live for him, every moment of every day. This is the purpose of my life."

To think about: Do you agree with the first man or the second man? Or maybe you have another purpose? What is the purpose of <u>your</u> life?

1   When we think about our lives it can become a burden for us. We get weighed down by our troubles in the present and our worries about the future. In the Holy Gospel (*Injil*) the Lord Jesus Christ made a wonderful promise which is for all of us:

> "Come to me, all you who are weary and burdened, and I will give you rest."
> (Matthew 11:28)

Think of Jesus Christ saying these words to you personally! Keep repeating them until you can say them from memory. Then fill in the gaps below:

"Come to me, all you who are _____ and _____, and I will give you rest."

2   The Lord Jesus Christ spoke these words when he came into the world. He called people to "come, follow me". Some of them responded with gladness and became his followers. Others rejected him. Christ is alive today and he still makes the same invitation to us. What is this? "Come, _____ me".

Come Follow Me

Becoming Jesus Christ's Follower

3   Let's learn how to become Christ's follower. We can follow the example of a fisherman named Simon Peter who was one of Christ's first followers. Let's read about this in the Holy Bible:

> One day as Jesus was standing by the Lake of Gennesaret, the people were crowding around him and listening to the word of God. He saw at the water's edge two boats, left there by the fishermen, who were washing their nets. He got into one of the boats, the one belonging to Simon, and asked him to put out a little from shore. Then he sat down and taught the people from the boat.
>
> When he had finished speaking, he said to Simon, 'Put out into deep water, and let down the nets for a catch'. Simon answered, 'Master, we've worked hard all night and haven't caught anything. But because you say so, I will let down the nets.'
>
> When they had done so, they caught such a large number of fish that their nets began to break... When Simon Peter saw this, he fell at Jesus' knees and said, 'Go away from me, Lord; I am a sinful man!' For he and all his companions were astonished at the catch of fish they had taken... Then Jesus said to Simon, 'Don't be afraid: from now on you will fish for people'. So they pulled their boats up on shore, left everything and followed him."
>
> (Luke 5:1-11 in the Holy Bible)

After you have read the whole passage, tick (✓) this box ☐ and continue.

4   It seems that Simon Peter took four steps to become Jesus' follower. By these same four steps people today become followers of the Lord Jesus. Let's learn about them now.

First Step: Turn away from Sin
When Simon saw the miracle of the fish, his eyes were opened. He recognized the Lord Jesus' holiness, and by contrast his own shame. What did he say to Jesus? "Go away from me, Lord; I am a _____" *(see the passage above, in the last paragraph)*

5   Simon realized he was a 'sinful man'. Probably he had never murdered anyone, or committed adultery. But Jesus could see right inside his heart. Simon could not hide from the Lord Jesus his shameful secrets or his evil thoughts.

What about you? What are your hidden secrets, which would make you die of embarrassment if they were announced aloud from the loudspeaker in your local mosque? Maybe you can hide these secrets from your neighbours and family, but you can't hide them from Jesus Christ. He can see every hidden evil in your life as clearly as a doctor can see, in an X-ray, every hidden bone of your body!

> ➢ *Pause now, and ask Jesus Christ to show you the dark corners of your life.*

6   Truly every person is stained by sin. As the poet Omar Khayum said,
       "Tell me who has not sinned in this world
          Tell me where are those who have not sinned,
          I wrong you and you wrong me
          So tell me what is the difference between you and me."

Can anyone hide his or her sins from God? [Yes / No] *(circle the correct answer)*

Lesson One

7   You were previously taught that God loves those who make themselves pure and hates those who do wrong. But did Jesus the Pure One hate the impure Simon? Astonishingly, he did not! What did Jesus say to Simon? *(see the passage in question 3 and tick the correct answer:)*

___ a) 'Go away from me'
___ b) 'Don't be afraid'

8   How relieved Simon was to hear Jesus say 'don't be afraid'! If you, like Simon, realize you are an impure sinner, then take heart. Jesus the Messiah gave his own life as a sacrifice for you, as Supplement 2 makes clear. He is ready to forgive you and wash you completely clean!

But are you ready to receive his generous gift? Look at these two contrasting people:

"I am a righteous person already, I need no help from Jesus"

"I know I am a sinner, I need Jesus to cleanse me"

Imran   ***Shafiq***

Which kind of person will Jesus Christ wash clean: a proud person like Imran or a humble one like Shafiq? _____

9   The Lord Jesus said 'I have come to call... *'sinners to repentance'* (Luke 5:32). 'Repentance' means turning around to go in the opposite direction. Look at these two men:

a) Which of these men has repented, 1. or 2.? ____

b) Which of them is continuing in his old ways, 1. or 2.? ____

1.   **2.**

10   'To repent' is more than merely to regret our sins. It means completely to <u>turn away from sin</u>, like man 2 in the picture. Therefore, what is the evidence of real repentance? *(tick one answer)*

___ a) to feel no regret for your sin-stained life
___ b) to regret your sins but not to change your lifestyle
___ c) to completely turn away from sin and change your lifestyle

11   What was the first step Simon took to become Jesus' follower? Turn away from _____.

3

Come Follow Me

Second Step: Understand the Cost

12   The next step for Simon was to understand the cost of becoming Christ's follower. Simon faced a hard choice. He was probably caught between two thoughts:

> If I become Christ's follower, I will receive forgiveness, peace of heart and the promise of paradise. I will know God personally and will serve Him joyfully.

> But as Christ's follower, I would also have to give up so much: my fishing business, my security, my old sinful life, maybe even my family!

What did Simon understand? The _____ of becoming Christ's follower.

13   Jesus Christ told this parable about how much it might cost to become his follower:

> "The kingdom of heaven is like a merchant looking for fine pearls. When he found one of great value, he went away and sold everything he had and bought it"   (Matthew 13:45-46)

As Jesus' follower, what are the most costly things you might have to give up? Tick one or more of the following: *(your own answer)*
    ___ a) your reputation in the community
    ___ b) your employment or business
    ___ c) your family
    ___ d) your property or inheritance
    ___ e) other *(write it here)* _____

14   But 'the pearl of great value' is worth it! And whatever sacrifice we made for Christ's sake, remember that he made an even bigger sacrifice for us on the cross!

> "God demonstrates his own love for us in this: While we were still sinners, Christ died for us"   (Romans 5: 8)

So, who paid the greater price: we or Christ? _____

In lessons 9 and 10 we will learn how Jesus Christ helps us to face persecution.

Lesson One

Third Step: Entrust yourself to Christ

15   To become Christ's follower, Simon had <u>firstly</u> to turn away from sin, and <u>secondly</u> to understand the cost. Then he came to the <u>third step</u>: "Entrust yourself to Christ".

In question 3, read again the last sentence in the passage. What did Simon and his companions do in response to Jesus' call? *(fill the blank spaces)*

"They pulled their boats up on shore, _____ everything and _____ him."

16   Simon entrusted himself completely to his new master Jesus.

How do we entrust ourselves to someone in everyday life? Here are some examples:
- ✓ *A tired child* entrusts himself to his father when he jumps into his arms to be carried.
- ✓ *A patient* entrusts himself to the doctor when he takes the medicine.
- ✓ *A passenger* entrusts himself to the bus driver at the start of a dangerous journey.

Just like the child, the patient or the passenger, we entrust ourselves to Jesus when we place ourselves in his hands. We trust him to protect and guide us. We obey him as our master.

What is the third step in becoming Christ's follower?
  1. Turn away from sin
  2. Understand the cost
  3. _____ yourself to Christ

17   After entrusting himself to Jesus Christ, Simon Peter travelled with him for the next three years. He shared in his master's joys and sorrows. He saw Jesus heal sick people and even raise the dead! He learned to love people as Jesus loved people. Gradually the apprentice Simon became more and more like his teacher Jesus. Later he was better known by his second name Peter.

How did Simon Peter become Christ's follower? *(tick the better answer)*
  ___ a) By entrusting himself to Christ
  ___ b) By reciting a new creed (*kalima* or *shahada*)

18   As you know, an apprentice learns from his master by watching and copying what he does. This is how Simon Peter developed as Jesus' apprentice or 'disciple'.

We too become like apprentices when we follow Jesus our master. Even though we cannot see him with our physical eyes, we learn to copy what he does and we become like him. We have the honour of sharing in his work.

What is the third step in becoming Christ's disciple? _____ yourself to Christ

Fourth Step: Join Christ's Community

19   When Simon obeyed Jesus' call, he was not alone. He <u>joined Christ's community</u>. Together Christ's disciples lived as one group and shared their lives. They were from different tribes and different social levels. But they learned to love each other.

This was not easy. Sometimes they had arguments. But they solved their disputes and forgave each other. Simon Peter learned that all those who belong to Christ must also join his _____.

Joining Christ's community is essential for every believer!
We will learn more in lesson 7.

Come Follow Me

20   Jesus Christ called Simon Peter to be his follower. What four steps did this involve?
   1. _____ from sin
   2. _____ the cost
   3. _____ yourself to Christ
   4. _____ Christ's community

Finally, what does today's lesson mean for you personally?

- *Maybe you are already Christ's follower?* If so, this course will help you to keep growing in Christ.

- *Maybe you are ready to become Christ's follower now?* Then talk in private with your advisor, and he or she will help you to take this step.

- *Maybe you want more time to think about this important step?* That's fine, but don't delay the decision forever, for one day it may be too late. Keep studying this course if you wish, but you will gain more benefit from it after you decide to follow Christ.

LESSON 1 PRACTICAL TASK

This week, find a place alone and think seriously about these questions. Are you already Christ's follower? Or are you ready to become his follower? Or do you want more time to think about it?

Now do the Review.

LESSON 1 REVIEW

1. What wonderful invitation of Jesus Christ did you memorize from Matthew 11:28? *(see question 1 if you can't remember)*

"Come to me, all you _____."

2. Name four steps in becoming Christ's follower:

   1. _____ from _____
   2. _____ the _____
   3. _____ yourself to _____
   4. _____ Christ's _____

LESSON 1 ANSWERS

1. weary, burdened
2. follow
3. read the passage
4. sinful man
5. personal response
6. No
7. b)
8. a humble person
9. a) person 2   b) person 1
10. c)
11. sin
12. cost
13. personal response
14. Christ
15. left... followed
16. entrust
17. a)
18. entrust
19. community
20. 1. turn   2. understand   3. entrust   4. join

Study tip: You can't study this course on your own. Find an advisor or a friend and discuss each lesson with him or her.

Lesson 2   New Life in Christ

> A person who becomes Christ's follower does not merely recite a new creed. Rather, he or she receives a brand new life in Christ! This includes:
> A. A new identity
> B. A new birth
> C. A new nature

1   Let's learn about this wonderful new life from a part of the Holy Bible called 'The First Letter of Peter', or 1 Peter for short. Simon Peter, about whom we learned in lesson 1, wrote this letter under God's guidance. The letter begins like this:

"Peter, an apostle of Jesus Christ"   (1 Peter 1:1)

What title does Peter have here? *(tick the correct answer)*
  ___ a) disciple   ___ b) apostle   ___ c) prophet

2   In the Holy Bible, the word 'apostle' means a person who is sent with a special task (not someone to whom a holy book descends). The Lord Jesus chose twelve men, trained them and sent them out with a special task. That is why they are called 'apostles'. Their leader was the apostle Peter.

Which part of God's Word will we study in this course? The first letter of the apostle _____

3   The first verse of 1 Peter tells us who wrote this letter under God's guidance. It also tells us who received the letter. They were followers of Christ living in the country we now call Turkey. In this verse they are called "God's chosen people" (*New Living Translation*).

> ➤ *Pause and thank God for making us his chosen people!*

4   The same verse also calls them "foreigners" (*NLT*). Maybe you live far from your homeland. Or maybe you still live in your country but you are separated from your family because they rejected you. This is a very hard experience!

But in God's sight, what new identity do we have? We are 'God's chosen _____'

A) Our New Identity
5   Yes, we are 'God's chosen people'! Our old community may reject us, but *"if God is for us, who can be against us?... Who will bring any charge against those whom God has chosen?"* (Romans 8:31,33). *"Will not God bring about justice for his chosen ones, who cry out to him day and night?"* (Luke 18:7)

As Christ's followers, what is our new identity? *(tick the correct answer)*
   ___ a) God's chosen people   ___ b) infidels   ___ c) apostates

6   The next verse says *"God the Father knew you and chose you long ago"* (1 Peter 1:2, *NLT*)

Lesson Two

> The story is told about a boy who had lost his real parents. Another couple brought him up as their own adopted son. One day other boys were mocking him about this. He replied, "No, I feel more honoured than you. Your fathers did not choose you but my father chose me as his very own!"

What an honour it is to be chosen by God! Did we deserve this by our good deeds?

[Yes / No]

7   God chose us because he loves us, not because we deserved it. It is also true that we chose to follow God through Jesus Christ. Somehow God's choice and our choice work together.

What is our new identity in Christ? We are God's _____ people.

B) Our New Birth

8   You know the difference between a worm and a caterpillar. Although they look rather similar, there is actually a huge difference between them. A worm crawls around without any change until it dies. But a caterpillar goes through a marvellous change. Instead of dying, what does it become? *(see the picture)*

_____

9   Isn't it a marvel that the ugly caterpillar, which merely crawled along a leaf, is changed into a beautiful butterfly which soars in the sky? It is like going through a completely 'new birth' to become a new creature.

What change takes place in the caterpillar? A kind of 'new _____ '

10   Have you become a follower of Jesus Christ? When you look in the mirror you see the same person as you were before, on the <u>outside</u>. But in fact, the change <u>inside</u> you is as great as a caterpillar becoming a butterfly. This amazing change through Christ is called 'new birth'.

Which people experience this new birth? *(tick one)*
   ___ a) all those who live in our country
   ___ b) all those who personally entrust themselves to Christ
   ___ c) all those who were born in a Christian family

11   The next verse of 1 Peter tells us about this new birth:

> "Praise be to the God and Father of our Lord Jesus Christ! In his great mercy he has given us <u>new birth</u> into a living hope through the resurrection of Jesus Christ from the dead"
>
> (1 Peter 1:3)

According to this verse, who has given us this new birth?
   ___ a) God in his great mercy
   ___ b) we by our good deeds
   ___ c) a holy man by his prayers for us

Come Follow Me

Have you experienced this New Birth?

12   God offers this new birth to everyone, but not everyone receives it.

Look at what the doctor says to the three patients, and their replies:

This medicine will make you better.

A. I believe you, doctor, but I won't take it.

B. I don't believe you! Leave me alone!

C. Give it to me please, doctor.

Which of these three sick people, A. B. or C. will get better? _____

13   In the same way, which of the three people below will receive new birth in Christ? *(tick one)*
   ___ a) The one who says, "I believe your teaching, O Christ, but I am afraid to receive you into my life"
   ___ b) The one who says, "I do not believe you"
   ___ c) The one who says, "I believe you, Lord Jesus. Now I entrust myself to you. Please come into my life".

Which one of these describes you – A., B. or C.? If you have not yet entrusted yourself to Christ, please talk about it in private with your advisor. The rest of this course assumes that you have taken this step.

C) Our New Nature

14   We have learned about our 'new identity' and 'new birth' as Christ's followers. Jesus Christ also gives us a 'new nature', which is his own nature in us.

Many people from the same previous religion as you have become Christ's followers. Here some of them describe the positive changes he has made in their lives:

Talib:	"Life in Christ is an exciting and soul-satisfying life"
Hasan:	"Jesus gave me joy and peace"
Shamim:	"My tension and worry disappeared"

Shaheeda:	"My burdens and fears have gone"
Lena:	"I know that God accepts me just as I am"
Ahmad:	"The colour of my past was black and its smell was of alcohol, women and sin. The colour of my present is light, covered with joy and peace"

(from 'Jesus More than a Prophet' by Ralph Wotton)

These are all real people. What difference came in their lives? *(tick one)*
___ a) Jesus Christ gave them a new nature with many positive changes
___ b) Their lives became worse than before
___ c) They were left unchanged in their old nature

15   Jesus Christ gave his new nature to all these his followers. Like them, we too will experience new <u>feelings</u> of joy and peace. But our feelings are not the most important thing. More important are the changes Jesus brings to our <u>character</u>. Here are some more true examples:

Hasan:	"Jesus enabled me to break my smoking habit"
Jehangir:	"Jesus changed my old attitude of pride"
Razzaq:	"My stammer and inferiority complex disappeared"
Saeed:	"I stopped being a troublemaker"
Shamim:	"I became more interested in other people"
Parwaiz:	"The spirit of service has taken the place of pride and conceit in my life"
Reza:	"I learned to rely on the Lord in my business and to work with honesty"
Mariah:	"I long to bring others to know Christ's love"

(from 'Jesus More than a Prophet' by Ralph Wotton)

What actual changes has Christ brought in your own life? Write your ideas, and be ready to share them in the discussion time: _____
_____
_____

16   If you have not immediately experienced all the above changes, don't worry. They will come gradually as you grow in Christ. It takes many years for a baby to grow into an adult, and in the same way it takes many years after receiving 'new birth' to become spiritually mature.

But because Jesus lives in you, which 'nature' should be seen more and more in you?
___ a) your old sinful nature   ___ b) your new nature in Christ

Our Spiritual Battle

17   Even though we already have a new nature in Christ, we must also fight a kind of spiritual war against our old nature - every day for the rest of our lives! God's Word gives us this command:

> "Now you must also rid yourselves of all such things as these: anger, rage, malice, slander and filthy language from your lips. Do not lie to each other, since you have <u>taken off</u> your old self [nature] with its practices and have <u>put on</u> the new self [nature], which is being renewed in knowledge in the image of its Creator."   (Colossians 3:5,7-10)

Come Follow Me

According to the above verses, *(put a circle round the correct answers)*
      a) which nature have we 'taken off'?   [old nature / new nature]
      b) which nature have we 'put on'?   [old nature / new nature]

18   The pictures below show Christ's followers doing different things. In the blank space by each name, write 'old' if the person is behaving according to their old nature, or 'new' for their new nature:

"I love other people more than before"

"Let me help you"

"I just can't stop drinking"

"You useless wife! You burnt the food again!"

Person a): _____ nature   Person b): _____ nature   Person c): _____ nature   Person d): _____ nature

19   Every day our new nature, which is Jesus' nature put into us, fights against our old sinful nature. A simple farmer once described this struggle like this: "I feel as if two goats are fighting in my life, a black one and a white one." His listener asked him, "So which goat wins?" He replied, "Whichever one I feed the most"!

> *Think about the farmer's parable. The black goat represents our old nature and the white goat our new nature. Which one is winning in your life these days? Why? Be ready for the discussion time.*

From today's lesson, let's remember three great privileges we have in Christ:
- We have a <u>new identity</u> as God's chosen people
- We have gone through a <u>new birth</u>, like a caterpillar becoming a butterfly
- With Christ's help, our <u>new nature</u> gradually replaces our old sinful nature

20   The following verse from God's Word summarizes what we have learned today:

> "If anyone is in Christ, he is a new creation; the old has gone, the new has come!"
> (2 Corinthians 5:17) *NIV 1984*

Fill the gaps and repeat the verse until you know it by heart:
"If anyone is in _____ , he is a _____ creation; the _____ has gone, the _____ has come!"
(2 Corinthians 5:17)

Now say this prayer:

> "O Lord,
> In your great mercy you made us your own chosen people – thank you!
> Thank you for giving me new birth and a new nature.
> By Christ's power, help me daily to fight the spiritual war against my old sinful nature.
> Amen."

LESSON 2 PRACTICAL TASK

Make a list of three positive changes in your life, which come from your new nature. Thank God for these changes. Also make a list of three habits from your old nature which still persist in your life. This week, with God's help, fight against these bad habits.

LESSON 2 REVIEW

1   a) When a person entrusts himself to Christ, what change takes place in him or her? _____ birth

    b) What new identity do we have as Christ's followers? We are God's _____ _____

2   Our spiritual battle is between our [old / new] sinful nature and our [old / new] nature in Christ *(cross out the wrong answers)*

3   Give two examples of changes which Jesus Christ brings in the life of his followers *(if you can't think of any, see questions 11-12)*:
    _____

4   From memory, fill the gaps from the verse 2 Corinthians 5:17:

    "If anyone is in _____ , he is a _____ creation; the _____ has gone, the _____ has come!"

Come Follow Me

LESSON 2 ANSWERS

1. b)
2. Peter
3. personal response
4. people
5. a)
6. No (but if you are not sure about this, talk with your advisor)
7. chosen
8. a butterfly
9. birth
10. b)
11. a)
12. C
13. c)
14. a)
15. be ready for discussion
16. b)
17. a) old nature   b) new nature
18. a) new   b) new   c) old   d) old
19. be ready for discussion
20. memorize the verse

Study tip: Don't rush through the course. Instead, put each lesson into practice before going to the next lesson.

14

Lesson 3   God the Father

In this course, you will read many true accounts about people who had the same previous religion as you. One of these was named Bilquis Sheikh.

Whenever Bilquis tried to reach out to God, he always seemed so far away. She could not communicate with him. Then one day a follower of Christ suggested to Bilquis, 'Try speaking to God as your Father'. At first she was horrified! This idea seemed to be *shirk* (associating something with God). But later she tried it. This is what happened:

" 'Oh Father, my Father'. Hesitantly, I spoke His name aloud... 'Father, oh my Father God', I cried, with growing confidence.... He was there! I could sense His Presence. I could feel His hand laid gently on my head. It was as if I could see His eyes, filled with love and compassion. He was so close that I found myself laying my head on His knees like a little girl sitting at her father's feet. For a long time I knelt there, sobbing quietly, floating in His love."

(from her book *'I Dared to Call Him Father'*)

So, is it blasphemy to call God our Father? Let's continue our study in 1 Peter chapter 1.

1   1 Peter 1:3 says:

"Praise be to the God and Father of our Lord Jesus Christ!" (1 Peter 1:3)

What title is used for God in this verse?
___ a) Lord   ___ b) Father   ___ c) Creator

2   Yes, God's names include not only *Rabb* (Lord) and *Khaliq* (Creator), but also 'Father'! Many people have heard 99 other names for God, but never this one. Yet Jesus Christ himself called God 'Father' and he even taught his followers to do the same.

By what title did Jesus speak to God? _____

A) Jesus Christ called God 'Father'

3   Many times in the New Testament we read that Jesus Christ spoke to God as 'Father' or even 'Abba' (which means 'Dad'). Some Jewish people were shocked by this. One time they tried to kill Jesus because *"he was even calling God his own Father, making himself equal with God"* (John 5:18).

Come Follow Me

Of what did they accuse Jesus? *(tick one)*
___ a) *shirk* (associating someone with God)   ___ b) murder   ___ c) theft

4   Let's read how Jesus Christ responded to these critics:

> "Whatever the Father does the Son also does. For the Father loves the Son and shows him all he does... Whoever does not honour the Son does not honour the Father, who sent him... For as the Father has life in himself, so he has granted the Son also to have life in himself. And he has given him authority to judge"   *(verses from John 5:19-27)*

In the box, put a circle round all the places where it says 'Son' or 'Father'.

5   Christ's followers are not embarrassed by these words 'Son' and 'Father' but we do need to explain them carefully. Does the passage above say anything at all about God having physical relations with a woman to produce a son? [Yes / No]

6   The idea of God having a physical union with a woman is very offensive to Christians! The Holy Bible never teaches anything like that! In fact, it uses the title 'son of God' for different beings including Adam, angels, the anointed king, and even the whole nation of Israel. They lived close to God, showed some of his qualities or ruled as his representatives on earth.

In what way could such creatures be called 'sons' of God? *(tick one)*
___ a) in a physical way, through union between God and a woman
___ b) in a descriptive way, to explain truths about them and God

7   In our everyday speech too, we use 'son' and 'father' in a descriptive way, not just a physical way. The founder of Pakistan is given the title 'father of the nation'. This does not mean that he physically gave birth to all the Pakistanis! In Afghanistan, a 'son of Herat' just means someone who belongs there. It is the same idea in Egypt when they call someone 'son of the Nile' – this does not mean that the Nile literally gave birth to this person.

When people talk about 'son' and 'father' do they always mean this in a physical way?
[Yes / No]

8   The words 'father' and 'son' are used in a descriptive way to show how Jesus Christ shared God's qualities and his authority. But Jesus Christ is the Son of God in an even greater way, in fact a unique way. He said *"Anyone who has seen me has seen the Father"* (John 14:9) !

We cannot see God with our own eyes, but he became visible on earth in Jesus Christ! Christ is somehow like an exact photocopy of God's nature. Therefore we can know the Father through knowing Jesus his Son.

a) Can anyone see the invisible God here on earth? [Yes / No]
b) Did God show himself on earth in Jesus Christ? [Yes / No]

9   We have learned a little about why Jesus Christ called God 'Father'. Don't worry if you don't understand it all, as we will learn more later.   To summarize:

a) By what title did Jesus speak to God? _____
b) In the Bible, is the term 'son of God' used in a physical or a descriptive way? _____
c) In whom did the invisible God become visible on earth? _____

Lesson Three

B) We too may call God 'Father'

10   Normally no one would dare to speak to the Almighty God as 'Father'. But Jesus Christ taught his followers to do that. And God's Word says,

> "See what great love the Father has lavished on us, that we should be called children of God! And that is what we are!" (1 John 3:1)

By what title do we dare to speak to God, through Jesus Christ? _____

11   Of course God does not have children in a physical way. Rather, God has adopted us as his spiritual sons and daughters. He has generously poured out ('lavished') his love on us!

Here again is the verse from question 10. Fill the blanks, and keep repeating the verse until you can say it from memory:

> "See what _____ _____ the Father has lavished upon us, that we should be called _____ of God! And that is what we are!" (1 John 3:1)

The character of our heavenly Father

12   No doubt your parents love you very much. But some parents show conditional love to their children. They love the child who brings them honour, but not the child who disappoints them. Or maybe it seems that your parents love your brother or sister more than you?

Our divine Father is not like that! His love is unconditional and unlimited. We don't have to earn it. He loves us just the same whether we come 'top of the class' or 'bottom of the class'!

Write 'True' or 'False' by the following statements:
        a) God our Father loves us if we do good and hates us if we do bad _____
        b) God our Father always loves us, whether we are good or bad _____
        c) We should love our own children even when they are bad _____

13   Some people don't like to think of God as 'Father' because their own human fathers were so bad. Sadly, some human fathers are addicted to alcohol, beat their wives and abuse their children in different ways. Some fathers abandon their families or never show love to their children.

I once heard about a human father who told his son to stand on a low wall. He said, "Now jump into my arms. Don't worry, I will catch you". But when the boy jumped, the father deliberately let him crash to the ground. Then he said "That is to teach you a lesson of life. The lesson is – never trust anyone!"

Is our Father God like that untrustworthy father? No! No! No!

> ➤ *Pause now, and think about your own human father:*
> *- Thank God for any good qualities in your human father.*
> *- Ask God to heal you from any hurts in your heart about your father.*
> *- Let God show you much he loves you as your perfect heavenly Father.*

> If you feel deep hurts about your human father, keep praying about this in the coming weeks, and ask another follower of Christ to pray with you.

Come Follow Me

14   A story is told about a man who had two sons. The younger son grew impatient living at home, for he wanted to see the world. So he asked his father to give him his inheritance even before he died (what an insult that was!). Then the son went far away, wasted his money on parties and expensive living, and became so poor that he even had to eat pigs' food. He was a disgrace to his family's name.

Finally he became so desperate that he decided to risk coming home and asking his father's forgiveness. How would you expect the father to react? In your opinion, do you think he would:

    ___ a) welcome his son with open arms?
    ___ b) reject him and send him away?
    ___ c) let him back into the home, but with a heavy punishment?

15   In fact, this story was first told by Jesus Christ, who continued in a surprising way:

> "But while [the son] was still a long way off, his father saw him and was filled with compassion for him; he ran to his son, threw his arms around him and kissed him. The son said to him, 'Father, I have sinned against heaven and against you. I am no longer worthy to be called your son.' But the father said to his servants, 'Quick! Bring the best robe and put it on him. Put a ring on his finger and sandals on his feet. Bring the fattened calf and kill it. Let's have a feast and celebrate. For this son of mine was dead and is alive again; he was lost and is found.' "
> (Luke 15:20-24)

a) What did the son deserve: to be welcomed or rejected? _____
b) But what did the father in Jesus' story actually do, welcome or reject his son? _____

16   By contrast, let me tell you about my friend Nazir (the account is true but I have changed his name).

> Around 1990 Nazir was sent by his father, a senior religious leader in Uganda, to study at a religious college (*madrassa*) overseas. But during that time Nazir became a follower of Christ.
>
> Several years later Nazir returned to his home in Uganda, hoping to be accepted by his father. Instead, from behind the locked gate, his father asked him 'We have heard rumours that you became a Christian – is it true?' 'Yes', Nazir admitted. 'Then you are no longer my son!', replied his father. Then, from behind the gate, he threw stones to drive Nazir away.
>
> Later Nazir told me, 'That day was the hardest day of my life'.

Which father is God like?
    ___ a) the father of Nazir, who rejected him because he brought dishonour
    ___ b) the father in Jesus' story, who welcomed his son even after he brought dishonour

17   We try not to cause dishonour to God our Father. But if we do, we must come back to him and apologize with our whole heart, like the son in Jesus' parable. When we do that, we can be sure the he will [never / probably] reject us. *(circle the correct answer)*

18   It is written *"Though my father and mother forsake me, the Lord will receive me"* (Psalm 27:10). Often we are emotionally closer to our mothers than to our fathers. But God's love for us is even stronger than our mother's love!

Which one of the following will definitely <u>never ever</u> reject us? *(tick one only)*
    ___ a) our father   ___ b) our mother   ___ c) God

Isn't it wonderful to know that our Father God loves us without limit and will never reject us!

Now say this prayer:

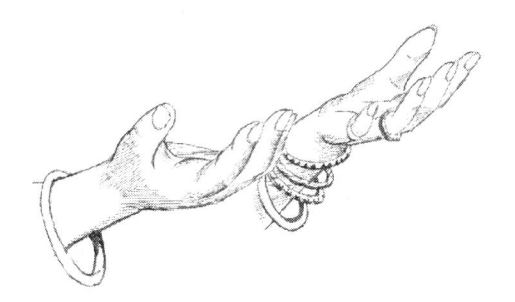

"Father God,
Thank you very much for adopting me as your spiritual child and loving me without limit. I too love you, and I want to bring you honour. Amen."

LESSON 3 PRACTICAL TASK

This week, think of two ways to show unconditional love to the members of your family and try to act on them.

For instance, how is your relationship with your father? Ask God to help you in this. How is your relationship with your children or your relative's children? Could you give them more time this week by paying attention to them and listening to what they want to tell you? Could you take them with you to the market, or give them a 'well done', or lovingly guide them to change a bad habit in their life?

Thank God that he always loves you unconditionally!

LESSON 3 REVIEW

1. a) By what title did Jesus Christ speak to God? _____
   b) Therefore, by what title do we dare to speak to God? _____

2. By each of the following statements, write 'True' or 'False':
   a) God our Father loves us even when we fail _____
   b) We can trust God our Father <u>all</u> the time _____
   c) God our Father will never reject us _____

3. Write the verse you memorized:

"See what _____ has _____ that we should be called _____ . And that _____!" (1 John 3:1).
(if you can't remember, see question 10)

Come Follow Me

LESSON 3 ANSWERS

1. b)
2. Father
3. a)
4. put a circle round 'Son' or 'Father' in the box
5. No
6. b)
7. No
8. a) No   b) Yes
9. a) Father   b) metaphorical   c) Jesus Christ
10. Father
11. great, love, children
12. a) False   b) True   c) True
13. your personal response
14. for the discussion time
15. a) rejected b) welcome
16. b)
17. never
18. c)

Study tip: Is your discussion leader using the Advisor Guide? It is helpful, and available free on the website.

Lesson 4   Obeying Christ by the power of his Spirit

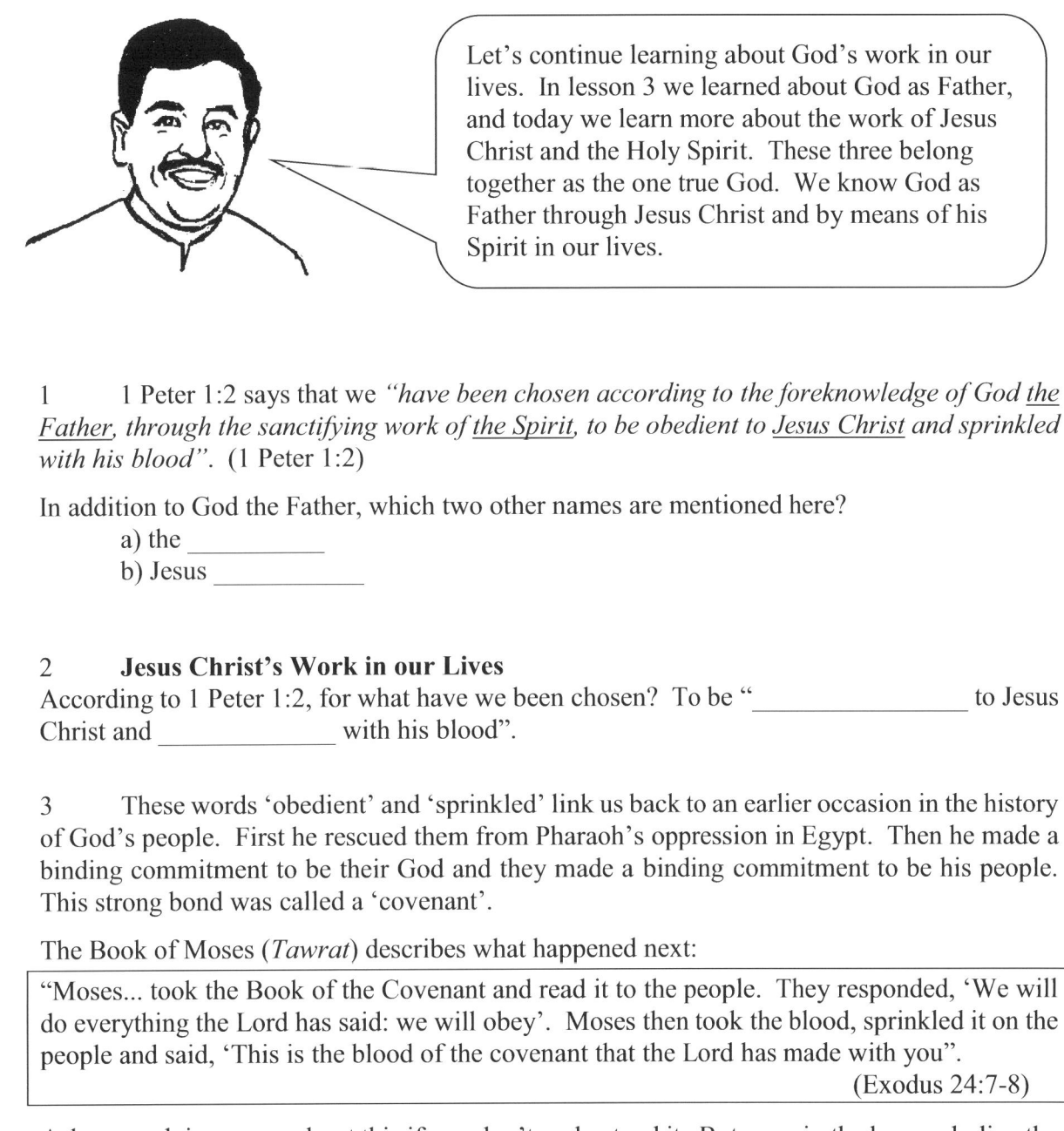

Let's continue learning about God's work in our lives. In lesson 3 we learned about God as Father, and today we learn more about the work of Jesus Christ and the Holy Spirit. These three belong together as the one true God. We know God as Father through Jesus Christ and by means of his Spirit in our lives.

1   1 Peter 1:2 says that we *"have been chosen according to the foreknowledge of God the Father, through the sanctifying work of the Spirit, to be obedient to Jesus Christ and sprinkled with his blood"*. (1 Peter 1:2)

In addition to God the Father, which two other names are mentioned here?
   a) the _____
   b) Jesus _____

2   **Jesus Christ's Work in our Lives**
According to 1 Peter 1:2, for what have we been chosen? To be "_____ to Jesus Christ and _____ with his blood".

3   These words 'obedient' and 'sprinkled' link us back to an earlier occasion in the history of God's people. First he rescued them from Pharaoh's oppression in Egypt. Then he made a binding commitment to be their God and they made a binding commitment to be his people. This strong bond was called a 'covenant'.

The Book of Moses (*Tawrat*) describes what happened next:

> "Moses... took the Book of the Covenant and read it to the people. They responded, 'We will do everything the Lord has said: we will obey'. Moses then took the blood, sprinkled it on the people and said, 'This is the blood of the covenant that the Lord has made with you".
> (Exodus 24:7-8)

Ask your advisor more about this if you don't understand it. But now, in the box underline the words 'obey' and 'sprinkled' and 'covenant'.

4   Moses shed the blood of an animal but Jesus Christ shed his own blood on the cross. He said *"this is my blood of the covenant, which is poured out for many for the forgiveness of sins"* (Matthew 26:28). His blood was poured out for us! Through the covenant, he is bonded to us and we are bonded to him. We are his people so we must obey him.

This bond is even stronger than the oath between a spiritual guide (*murshid*) and his disciple (*murid*).

According to 1 Peter 1:2,
a) whose blood is sprinkled on us as a seal of this covenant? _____
b) whom have we made a firm commitment to obey? _____

5   The pictures below show three of Christ's followers:

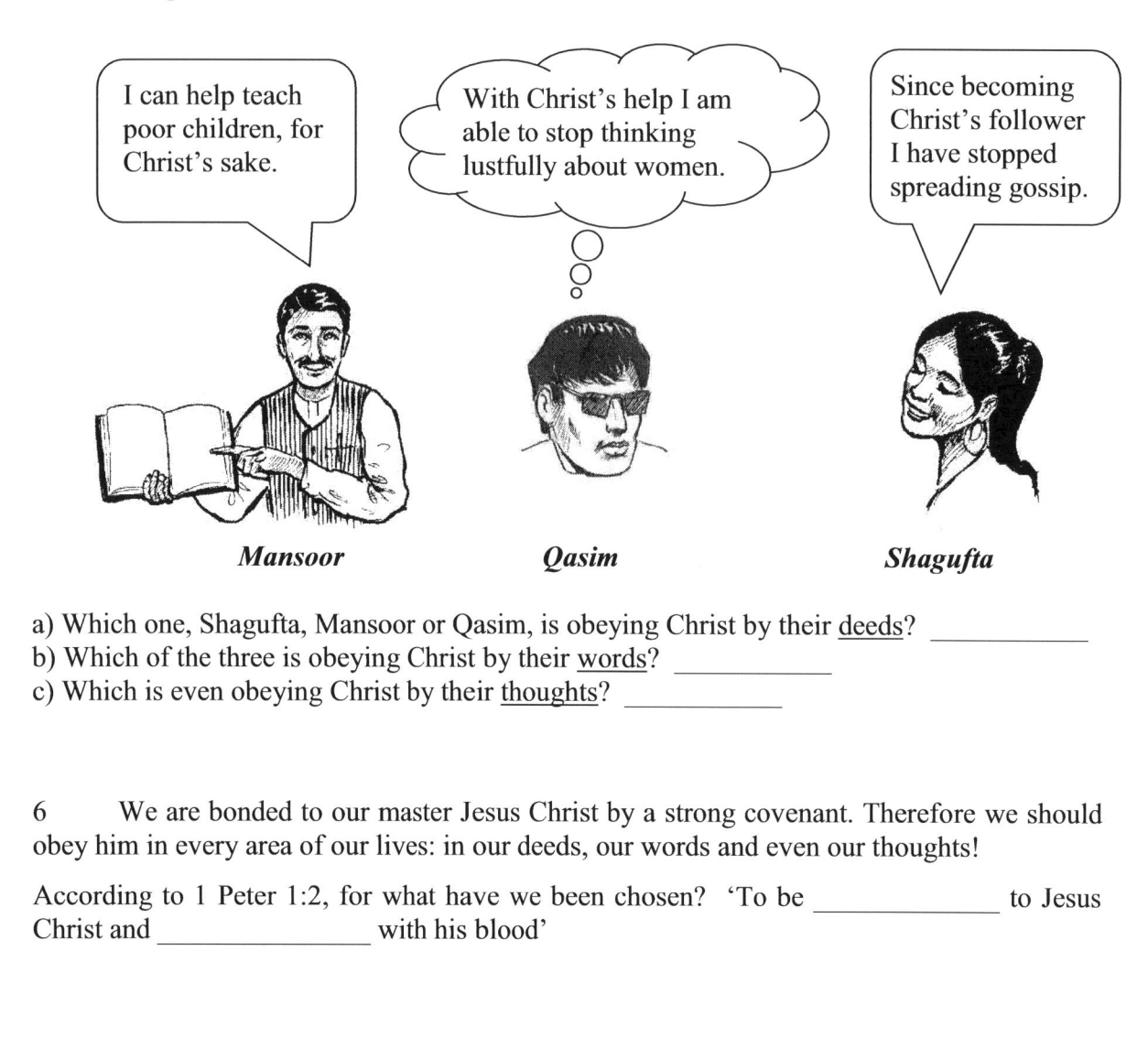

> I can help teach poor children, for Christ's sake.

> With Christ's help I am able to stop thinking lustfully about women.

> Since becoming Christ's follower I have stopped spreading gossip.

Mansoor   ***Qasim***   ***Shagufta***

a) Which one, Shagufta, Mansoor or Qasim, is obeying Christ by their <u>deeds</u>? _____
b) Which of the three is obeying Christ by their <u>words</u>? _____
c) Which is even obeying Christ by their <u>thoughts</u>? _____

6   We are bonded to our master Jesus Christ by a strong covenant. Therefore we should obey him in every area of our lives: in our deeds, our words and even our thoughts!

According to 1 Peter 1:2, for what have we been chosen? 'To be _____ to Jesus Christ and _____ with his blood'

The Holy Spirit's Work in our Lives

7   What gives us the inner strength to obey our master Jesus? 1 Peter 1:2 gives us the answer. It is 'the sanctifying work of the _____' *(see question 1 again)*

8   Let's find out more about 'the Spirit' mentioned here and many times in the Holy Bible. He is also called:
- the Spirit of God
- the Spirit of Christ
- the Holy Spirit.

This Holy Spirit is God's own personal presence, active in the world and especially in Christ's followers. So, according to the Bible's teaching, who is the Holy Spirit? *(tick one answer)*
   ___ a) the angel Gabriel
   ___ b) the personal presence of God, through Christ
   ___ c) an impersonal force like fate

Lesson Four

9   How do God the Father, Jesus Christ and the Holy Spirit belong together? God is the unique Creator, so no human language can properly explain him. But we see many created things which are 'three-in-one'.

For example, think about yourself as a human. You consist of body, mind and soul. Answer the questions below according to your own opinion and be ready for discussion:

a) How many individuals are you?   [One / Three]
b) Of how many parts do you consist?   [One / Three]
c) When all three parts work in harmony, are you a complete person?   [Yes / No]
d) If you just had a body and soul but no mind would you be complete?   [Yes / No]

> In some ways we humans reflect our Creator. Therefore, if the creatures have a three-in-one nature, could it be possible that their Creator also has a three-in-one nature? What do you think?

10   Here is another example which might help us understand the idea of three-in-one.

We are separated from the sun by a vast gap. We cannot cross that gap by our own efforts. If the sun kept itself separate without revealing anything, we could know nothing about it.

However, thankfully the sun does not keep to itself. It sends out its rays. The rays cross the vast gap; they reveal the sun to us and show us what it is like.

The rays fill our bodies with heat. This heat gives us life and strength.

We can distinguish between the sun, the rays and the heat, but we cannot tear them apart. They belong together as three-in-one..

What are three elements of the one sun? _____ , _____ and _____

11   Even greater than the gap between the sun and the earth, is the gap between the Creator and his creatures. But thankfully, God the Son crossed that vast gap when he came to this earth as Jesus Christ. He revealed God the Father to us. And God the Holy Spirit fills us with life and strength.

a) If the sun did not give rays and heat, could you see or feel it at all?   [Yes / No]
b) If the Father had not sent his Son and his Spirit, could you know God at all? [Yes / No]

> These examples help us to a limited extent. But by human logic we cannot fully understand the idea of God as three-in-one. Instead, God's Spirit assures us it is true. More important than *understanding* this truth is to *experience* the one true God as Father, Son and Spirit!

Come Follow Me

Some people find this diagram helpful. Come back to it in the discussion time if you wish.

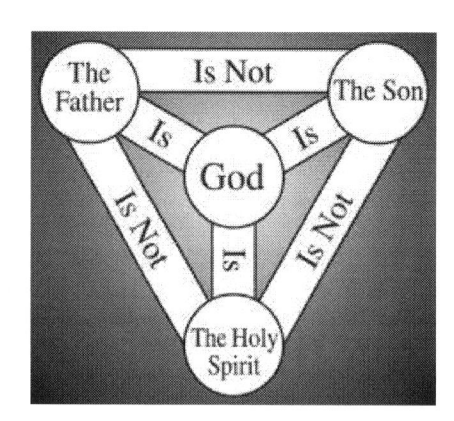

12   The Holy Spirit enables us to live for Christ. Without him we can do nothing. We will see this again and again throughout this course. The Holy Spirit enables us to:
- turn away from sin (lesson 1)
- receive a new life (lesson 2)
- talk with God and read his Word (lessons 5, 6)
- witness to others (lesson 13)
- follow Christ's straight path (lesson 15)
- serve one another, using his gifts (lesson 19)

So, to live as Christ's followers, is it 'essential' or 'optional' for his Holy Spirit to be active in our lives? _____

The Holy Spirit makes us holy

13   We read earlier from 1 Peter 1:2 about "the sanctifying work of the Spirit". To 'sanctify' means 'to set apart as holy'. God wants to set apart his people from a sin-stained lifestyle, in order to be dedicated to him alone.

Suppose you want to clean a dirty glass, to set it apart for the sole use of your special guest. With what would you clean it? *(tick one)*
    ___ a) with pure clean water   ___ b) with dirty water   ___ c) with alcohol

14   Of course, we use pure clean water to wash a dirty cup and set it apart for special use. God's Spirit is 'holy'. So he works in our life to make us holy and to set us apart for God's sole use. 1 Peter chapter 1 tells us more about this:

> "As obedient children, do not conform to the evil desires you had when you lived in ignorance. But just as he who called you is holy, so be holy in all you do; for it is written: 'Be holy, because I am holy'." (1 Peter 1:14-16)

In the box, underline all the places where it says 'holy'. How many did you find? ___

15   This passage sets an extremely high standard for us. God himself calls us to be holy in <u>all</u> we do! He calls us to be holy and pure just as he himself is!
a) Is it ever possible for us to reach this high standard in our own strength? _____
b) But who can make us holy? The Holy _____

16   Now let's memorize this verse:

> "But just as he who called you is holy, so be holy in all you do" (1 Peter 1:15)

Tick the box when you can say the verse without looking at the page. ☐

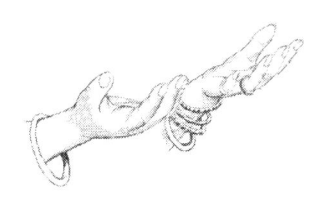

Lesson Four

This verse is easy to memorize but very hard to obey! Right now, ask God to fill you more and more with his Holy Spirit to make you holy.

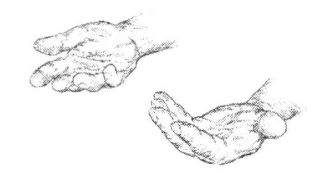

The Holy Spirit fills our lives

17   When Jesus Christ comes in to our lives, he lives in us not in a physical form, but by his Spirit.

a) Did you invite Jesus Christ to enter your life?   [Yes / No]
b) If 'yes', then do you have the Holy Spirit in your life?   [Yes / No]

18   All Christ's followers have his Spirit in their lives. In the Bible, one description of the Holy Spirit is like water. Look at these two glasses:

1.    *2.*

a) Which glass, 1. or 2., is like a person who never received Christ's Spirit in their life? __

b) Which glass, 1. or 2., is like a person who has the Holy Spirit in their life? __

19   But I want to be full to the brim with God's Spirit.

➢   I want to be holy as God is holy!

➢   I want to love him with <u>all</u> my heart!

➢   I don't want any dirty sin left in my life!

➢   *How about you? Do you want this too?*

Write your personal response here _____

20   As followers of Christ, we are so glad that his Spirit is in us.

    But every day we sin, and grieve the Holy Spirit within us, so every day we need to be again cleansed and set apart for God's sole use. We ask God to fill us so full with his Spirit that we overflow to refresh the people around us.

(Circle the correct answers:)
a) Whose work is it to cleanse and fill us afresh every day?
            [our own work / the Spirit's work]

b) Whose work is it to turn every day from sin and ask God to fill us afresh?   [our own work / the Spirit's work]

25

LESSON 4 PRACTICAL TASK

Do you long to be holy as God is holy?
Do you want to obey Christ by the power of his Spirit?
Do you want to become more like Jesus Christ each day?

These things are only possible through the Holy Spirit working in your life. Each day this week, when you wake up in the morning ask God to fill you afresh with his Spirit. Before going to sleep think about one way that God's Spirit worked in your life today.

Keep pressing on to 'be holy in all you do'. But don't despair when you fall short. His Holy Spirit works very patiently in your life. Over time you will see big changes from before!

<u>Please Note</u>: Starting from lesson 6, you will look up verses yourself in God's Word, instead of just reading them in this course book. So you must obtain your own copy of the Holy Bible.

The original languages of the Bible are Greek and Hebrew. But we understand its meaning with the help of different translations in English. In this course we use the New International Version (NIV 2011). If you already have a different translation that is fine. But the words may vary just a little because it is only a translation, not the original.

LESSON 4 REVIEW

1. We are bonded to our master Jesus Christ by a strong covenant. Therefore in what areas of our lives should we obey him? *(tick one or more correct answers)*

   ___ a) our deeds   ___ b) our words   ___ c) our thoughts   ___ d) all areas

2. According to the Bible's teaching, who is the Holy Spirit? *(tick one)*
   ___ a) the angel Gabriel
   ___ b) the personal presence of God, through Christ
   ___ c) an impersonal force like fate

3. Write the memory verse:
   "But just as _____ " (1 Peter ___ : ___)

4. What does this glass represent? *(tick one)*

   ___ a) a person who has never received Christ in their life

   ___ b) a person who is fully under Christ's control and overflowing with his Spirit

LESSON 4 ANSWERS

1. a) Spirit b) Christ
2. obedient, sprinkled
3. underline the words in the verse
4. a) Jesus Christ b) Jesus Christ
5. a) Mansoor b) Shagufta c) Qasim
6. obedient, sprinkled
7. Spirit
8. b)
9. For discussion. My personal opinion is a) One, b) Three, c) Yes, d) No. Your opinion may be different.
10. sun, rays, heat
11. a) No b) No (but if your answers are different bring them to the discussion)
12. essential
13. a)
14. 'holy' is mentioned four times
15. a) No b) Spirit
16. memorize the verse
17. a), b) personal answers
18. a) 1 b) 2
19. personal response
20. a) the Spirit's work b) our own work

Study tip: If you don't understand everything in this course, don't worry. Just obey the parts you do understand.

Lesson 5 Talking with God

1	Imagine a man trying to present his problem before a great king. He cannot enter the king's presence directly, instead he must deal with the servants.

But if the king's own daughter has a problem, she may come close to the king at any time. What gives her the right to do this? Of course, it is because she is the king's own child.

As we learned in lesson 3, you have the right to call God your Father! Therefore, how may you enter into his presence? (*tick one*)

___ a) directly, at any time
___ b) indirectly, through holy men
___ c) just at fixed times during the day

Talking with God as Father
2	1 Peter 1:17 reminds us that we 'call on a Father'. What will a loving father do when his daughter comes to talk with him?
	___ a) send her away
	___ b) tell her to contact his servant instead
	___ c) listen to her with patience and full attention

3	When we come close to our heavenly Father, he listens to us with patience and full attention. He is always willing to give us time. He wants us to come close to him. We do not need holy men to bring us close to God, instead we can directly enter his presence.

Circle 'true' or 'false' in the following statements:
	a) Our Father God wants us to come close to him		[True/False]
	b) We need to come to God through holy men		[True/False]
	c) Our Father God is always ready to listen to us		[True/False]

4	A loving father or mother wants their children to talk with them about anything. In the same way, we may talk with our loving father God about anything. Which things in the following list may we talk with God about? *(tick one or more)*

	___ our worries ___ our fears ___ our sorrows ___ our joys
	___ our sins ___ our families ___ our desires ___ our regrets

5	Yes, God wants us to talk with him about all these things! Jesus taught his followers to speak to God as 'dear father'.

How can we live close to God? By talking with him as our dear _____

Ritual or Personal Prayer?

6   When we talk with God as Father we don't need to use long words in a religious language. Christ's followers talk with God in their mother-tongue, with simple words. Is this more like the ritual prayer (*salah* or *namaz*) you are accustomed to, or like personal prayer (*dua*)? _____

7   We may talk with our heavenly Father at any time in any place, at any time. This is more like *dua* (personal prayer) than ritual prayer.

But prayer is not merely asking God for things. Above all, prayer is <u>talking with God</u>. We speak with him and he listens. He speaks with us and we listen.

a) What is prayer? _____ with God.
b) Does talking with our heavenly Father also include listening to him? [Yes / No]

8   Which answer below is the best description of Christian prayer? *(tick one only)*
    ___ a) talking with God as Father
    ___ b) doing ritual prayers
    ___ c) merely asking God for things

9   In prayer our motive is not to gain a religious reward. In fact our highest motive is not even to ask God to give us things. Above all, we pray in order to come close to God.

What should be our highest motive in prayer? To come _____ to God

10   Our hearts long to come close to God. Many poets wrote about how much they longed to experience this after their death. But through Christ, we can enjoy God's closeness right now in this life!

> "Though you have not seen him, you love him; and even though you do not see him now, you believe in him and are filled with an inexpressible and glorious joy" (1 Peter 1:8)

> ➢ *Stop now to thank God for the 'inexpressible and glorious joy' which he gives you through Christ. Ask him to help you live ever closer to him.*

Pray Continually

11   Probably you think that talking with God as Father is easier than doing the ritual prayers because it requires less effort. In one way, this is true. But in another way, it is harder! God's Word commands us to

> "Pray continually"   (1 Thessalonians 5:17)

Which is harder, to pray five times a day or to pray continually? _____

12   What does 1 Thessalonians 5:17 command us to do? _____

13   To 'pray continually' sounds impossible! But remember that the highest purpose of prayer is to come close to God. By means of his Spirit within us, we can do this all day long. A follower of Jesus from the same previous religion as you, explained it like this: *"When I pray, inside me I am praising and enjoying God, because there is something new in me, which is God's Spirit in contact with my spirit".*

Come Follow Me

So you can talk with God and listen to him in your heart, without speaking words aloud. Which of the following times offer a good opportunity for you to stay close to God, during your busy day? *(Tick one or more, according to your own circumstance)*

    ___ while sitting in a bus
    ___ while waiting in a queue
    ___ while walking to the market
    ___ while washing the dishes
    ___ before each meal

> Although we may talk with our heavenly Father at any time and any place, it is also very important to make a daily routine for personal prayer. This builds a healthy habit in our lives. We will discuss this further in the next lesson.

The Lord's Prayer

14   Jesus Christ taught his followers to use a prayer which we call 'the Lord's Prayer'. All over the world, Christ's followers say this prayer in their own languages:

> "Our Father in heaven,
> Hallowed be your name,
> Your kingdom come, your will be done, on earth as it is in heaven.
> Give us today our daily bread.
> And forgive us our debts, as we also have forgiven our debtors,
> And lead us not into temptation but deliver us from the evil one.
> For yours is the kingdom, the power and the glory. Amen"

After saying this prayer aloud twice, tick the box. ☐

15   The Lord's Prayer contains an ocean of meaning in a few simple words. We do not recite it to seek a reward, but because it gives us a good pattern for our own prayers. It reminds us of three kinds of prayer:
- <u>apologizing</u> to God
- <u>thanking</u> God
- <u>requesting</u> God

With whom do we talk, using these different kinds of prayer? _____

16   Let's think about these three kinds of prayer, in turn.

Apologizing

Suppose your son threw a ball inside the house, broke a window, and then demanded money from you to buy sweets. How would you feel? Too often we come to our heavenly Father like that! We ask him for things without even saying 'sorry' first.

Therefore, before asking for things, we should first confess our wrong deeds, wrong words and wrong thoughts which caused pain to our Father God.

What is the first kind of prayer we have mentioned?
    ___ a) apologizing   ___ b) thanking   ___ c) requesting

17   When we apologize to God for the ways we have dishonoured him, he keeps his promise to forgive us and cleanse our sin-stained consciences. Saying sorry is like a kind of spiritual cleansing (*wudu*) when we enter God's presence.

Put a circle round the correct answers below:
a) What does washing with water cleanse?   [our dirty bodies / our guilty consciences]
b) What does God cleanse when we confess our sins?
                                         [our dirty bodies / our guilty consciences]

Thanking
18   Often we come to God with a selfish motive, asking him to meet our own needs. But, as grateful children, shouldn't we also thank our heavenly Father for all he has done for us? He has given us salvation and so many physical and spiritual blessings.

What is this second kind of prayer? _____

19   We thank God not only for what he has done, but also for his own character. He is our loving, faithful, holy Redeemer! We praise him for being so wonderful. Write one characteristic of God which is very precious to you. _____

Requesting
20   Jesus said to his followers,

> "Which of you, if his son asks for bread, will give him a stone? Or if he asks for a fish, will give him a snake? If you, then, though you are evil, know how to give good gifts to your children, how much more will your Father in heaven give good gifts to those who ask him!"
> (Matthew 7:9-11)

Is our Heavenly Father glad or reluctant to give us good gifts when we ask him? _____

21   God loves to give his children good gifts. Therefore we come to him with all our requests. What kind of prayer is this? *(tick the correct answer)*

   ___ a) apologizing   ___ b) thanking   ___ c) requesting

22   We may ask God not only for our own needs, but also for the needs of whom? *(tick one or more, according to your own opinion)*

   ___ our family members
   ___ our friends cut off from Christ
   ___ the sick and needy
   ___ our government and leaders
   ___ our brothers and sisters in Jesus
   ___ our enemies
   ___ other: _____

Come Follow Me

Summary

23   Look at these three people using the three types of prayer:

"Father, thank you for being so generous! I love you!"

"Father, sorry I told a lie to my boss"

"O God, please help me to love my sister-in-law"

Shazia   *Nabeel*   *Firoza*

Draw lines to match each person with their related type of prayer *(the first line is already drawn for you, now do the others)*:

Person	Type
Firoza	apologizing
Nabeel	thanking
Shazia	requesting

Your personal response

Finally, using this prayer of the prophet David, ask your Father God to keep you always close to Him:

"My heart says of you, 'Seek his face!' Your face, Lord, I will seek" (Psalm 27:8)

LESSON 5 PRACTICAL TASK

Memorize the Lord's Prayer and speak it out in prayer each day this week. Be ready to say it in the group next week.

Also, try this list as a way to pray for different people each day this week:

Day	People I will pray for
Friday	My close family members
Saturday	My wider family and relatives
Sunday	Followers of Jesus in my country & worldwide
Monday	My friends who do not know Jesus
Tuesday	Any poor and sick people I know
Wednesday	The government and leaders of my country
Thursday	Christ's kingdom to spread around the world

LESSON 5 REVIEW

1. Which answer below is the best description of Christian prayer? *(tick one only)*
   ___ a) talking with God as Father
   ___ b) doing the ritual prayers
   ___ c) merely asking God for things

2. What three kinds of prayer have we learned in this lesson? *(see question 15)*
   _____ , _____ , _____

3. What does 1 Thessalonians 5:17 command us to do? _____ _____
   (see question 11)

4. Write here the Lord's Prayer *(if you haven't yet memorized it, copy it from question 14)*

   "Our Father, _____
   _____
   _____
   _____ "

> If you do not yet have your own copy of the Bible, please obtain one. You will need it for all the remaining lessons.

LESSON 5 ANSWERS

1. a)
2. c)
3. a) True b) False c) True
4. we may talk with God about all of these
5. father
6. personal prayer
7. a) talking b) Yes
8. a)
9. close
10. stop and pray about this
11. personal response
12. pray continually
13. share your answer in discussion
14. repeat the prayer twice, then continue reading
15. God our Father
16. a)
17. a) our dirty bodies b) our guilty consciences
18. thanking
19. personal response
20. glad
21. Asking
22. share your answer in discussion
23. Firoza – requesting, Nabeel – apologizing, Shazia - thanking

Lesson 6 God's Word for Us

In the last lesson we learned that one way to stay close to our heavenly Father is by talking with him. Another way is when he speaks to us through his Word, the Holy Bible.

Thirsty for God's Word

1   Look at these two babies and read their thoughts:

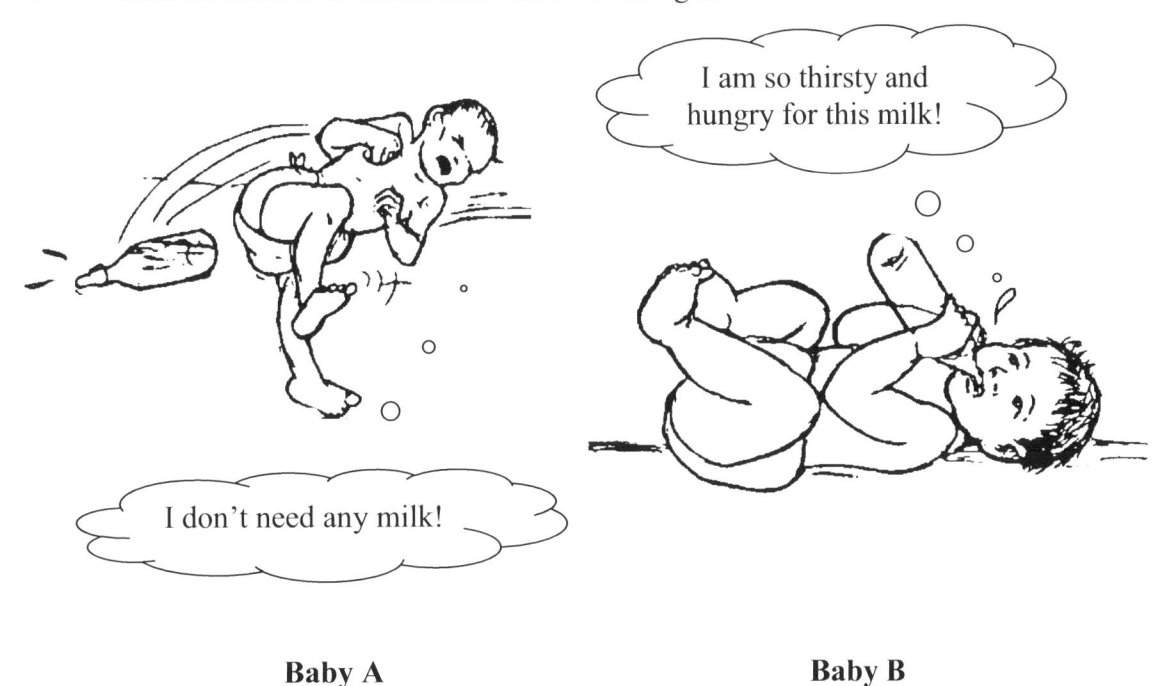

I am so thirsty and hungry for this milk!

I don't need any milk!

Baby A   **Baby B**

Which baby, A. or B., will grow strong and healthy? Baby _____

2   Of course, the foolish baby who says "I need no milk" will grow weak and die. Only those who are thirsty for pure, good milk will grow strong. 1 Peter tells us:

"Like newborn babies, crave pure spiritual milk, so that by it you may grow up in your salvation, now that you have tasted that the Lord is good."   (1 Peter 2:2-3)

Tasting one drop of milk will make a baby long for more.
a) Have you personally 'tasted that the Lord is good'? _____
b) Are you personally thirsty for 'pure spiritual milk' from God? _____

3   When we 'crave' something it means we long for it and yearn for it with all our heart. Hopefully we all crave for more and more from God, now that we have "tasted that the Lord is good"! But what is this 'pure spiritual milk' mentioned in the verse? Another translation is 'pure milk of the word'. Therefore, what does this phrase probably refer to?
       ___ a) cow's milk   ___ b) goat's milk   ___ c) the milk of God's Word

Come Follow Me

4   Like newborn babies, we should be thirsty for the pure milk of God's Word. A baby who does not crave for milk will not grow physically strong. And if Christ's followers do not crave the spiritual milk they will not grow spiritually strong.

What is this spiritual milk? God's _____

5   Read 1 Peter 2:2-3 again in question 1, and fill in the gaps:

"Like newborn babies, _____ pure spiritual _____, so that by it you may _____ up in your salvation, now that you have tasted that the Lord is good."

The Holy Bible is God's Word

6   God's Word, the spiritual milk which makes us grow strong, is the Holy Bible. Through the Bible God speaks to us. The Bible is God's Word in human language. It says,

> "Prophecy never had its origin in the human will, but prophets, though human, spoke from God as they were carried along by the Holy Spirit"   (2 Peter 1:21)

According to this verse, how did prophecy come? '_____, though human, spoke from ____'

7   According to the verse you have just read, answer the following 'True' or 'False':

a) Prophets invented their own words and pretended they came from God _____
b) Prophets spoke from God as they were carried along by the Holy Spirit _____

8   The prophets, and all the humans who wrote down different parts of the Bible, "spoke from God as they were carried along by the Holy Spirit". God breathed his thoughts into the writers' minds. They wrote his words by means of his Spirit. We trust the Bible as the 'Word of God'.

Nevertheless God did not treat the writers like machines or robots. He let them express his true message according to their culture and personality, but still under his own control and guidance.

How was God's Word written? "Prophets spoke from _____ as they were carried along by the Holy _____ "

9   Why do we call the Bible the Word of God? Because: *(tick one)*
        ____ a) It speaks just about God and nothing else
        ____ b) The writers spoke from God as they were carried along by his Spirit
        ____ c) It is the copy of a book in heaven
        ____ d) It was dictated by the angel Gabriel

10   God wants to communicate with all people, not just with those who can learn a special religious language. So God caused the Bible to be written in the ordinary human languages of Hebrew and Greek. Up till now, by God's help, parts of the Bible have been translated into more than 2500 languages! Some languages, like English, have several translations.

What does this show about God? *(tick one)*

        ____ a) He wants us to understand his Word in our own mother-tongue
        ____ b) He wants us to recite his Word in a special religious language

Lesson Six

The Different Parts of the Bible

11   By now you should have obtained your own copy of the Holy Bible.

Please open your Bible at the first page, 'List of Contents'. You will notice that the Bible consists of not just one book, but a library of 66 books. These are found in two main sections. The first is called the 'Old Testament'. What is the other section called? The '_____ Testament'. *(check the List of Contents)*

12   The **Old Testament** includes the *Tawrat* (Books of Moses), the *Zabur* (Psalms), and some other books. In the Old Testament we read how God Almighty got involved in human history. God created people, he spoke with them, he felt their pain and rescued them, he even came to meet them personally! He made promises to his prophets such as Noah, Abraham, Moses and David, and he gave a special task to the people of Israel.

Which Testament, Old or New, contains the *Tawrat* (Books of Moses) and *Zabur* (Psalms) alongside other books? _____

13   Perhaps you think it strange that much of the holy Bible describes humans and their activities, not just words from God himself. But actually this is God's chosen way. Instead of staying remote from men and women, he got closely involved in their lives.

So what does the Bible teach us about the Almighty Creator? *(tick one)*
   ___ a) He remained far off in heaven and sent his commands for us to obey
   ___ b) He came close to humans and got involved in their lives

14   In the **New Testament** we read how the Creator became even more closely involved in human affairs by entering this world in Jesus Christ! The Lord Jesus is the central theme of the New Testament: from when he first came to this earth as a baby, until he will come again on the Judgment Day.

Some people falsely think Christians wrote the New Testament as a 'new' book to replace the Old Testament. This is not true. Rather, the Old Testament tells the first part of the story and the New Testament is the second part of the same story.

a) Which Testament, Old or New, covers the period from the beginning of creation up until the coming of Jesus Christ? _____
b) Which Testament, covers the period from the first coming of Jesus Christ up until his second coming? _____
c) Does the New Testament replace the Old Testament, or continue it? _____

15   Each book of the Bible is divided up into chapters and verses. Bible references are always given in this order: first <u>book</u>, then <u>chapter</u>, then <u>verse</u>. This enables you to find any particular verse.

   Let's try this with the first epistle of Peter, also written as 1 Peter. Use the 'List of Contents' to find 1 Peter (near the end of the New Testament). Open your Bible at 1 Peter chapter 1. The chapter numbers are written in large font, and the verse numbers in smaller font.

Now find 1 Peter chapter 1 verse 3 and write the first three words here:
_____

Come Follow Me

> It is good to gain knowledge about the Bible. But it is even more important to let God speak to us through the Bible! For this, it helps very much to dedicate a particular time with God every day. Let's learn about that now.

A Daily Time with God

16   How often does a baby need milk? Once a month, once a week or every day? _____

17   Yes, a baby definitely needs milk every day. God's Word is our spiritual milk. Without it we will quickly become weak. Therefore, preferably, how often should we read it or listen to it? *(tick one)*

    ___ a) once a month   ___ b) once a week   ___ c) every day

18   To benefit from this spiritual milk, it is good to dedicate a special time at least once a day. Try to find a place and a time where you can be alone with God to read his Word. If you do not have privacy for this in your own home, then ask God to show you another place.

a) What is the best time for you each day to read the Bible without interruption? _____
b) What is the best place for you to read the Bible without interruption? _____

(Write your personal response, and be ready for the discussion time.)

19   Each day during your special time with your Lord, we suggest the following three steps to give you a routine:

Step 1:   **Prepare**

- Remember you are unclean, coming close to your pure Lord. So confess your sin, apologize to God and ask him to cleanse you.
- Then ask God to speak with you through his Word and help you understand it.

What is the first suggested step in your daily time with God? *(tick one)*
    ___ a) prepare   ___ b) read   ___ c) pray

20   After your heart is prepared and your conscience cleansed, go to step 2:

Step 2:   **Read**

- Start at the beginning of one book of the Bible, for instance 1 Peter or another book suggested by your advisor. Read a few verses or half a chapter.
- Stop at a verse which especially leaves its impression on you. You feel in your heart that God is especially speaking to you through that verse. It may be a truth about God, a promise to assure you, an example to follow, or a command to obey.

> To help you remember what God tells you, underline the words or write them in a notebook.
> It is good to memorize special verses. Someone may take away your written Bible, but no one can snatch God's Word from your memory. Memorized verses stay safe in your memory, change your thoughts and comfort your heart.
> Place a book-mark in the passage, to mark where to continue reading tomorrow with the next section.

What is the second step we suggest for your daily time with God?
___ a) prepare   ___ b) read   ___ c) pray

21   After reading your Bible for a few minutes, our suggested third step is this:

Step 3:   **Pray**

> Thank your Lord for his message to you through this verse and ask him to help you put it into practice.
> Talk with God about anything you like, using your own words, or the Lord's Prayer or another set prayer.
> Enjoy God's sweet close presence!

What three steps do we suggest for your daily time with God?
   Step 1: _____
   Step 2: _____
   Step 3: _____

22   If your family members are followers of Jesus, you may *prepare*, *read* and *pray* all together, instead of doing it on your own. Or if you have a close friend who loves Jesus, you can meet with him/her regularly, to explore God's Word together and support each other in prayer.

What is the best way for you to spend a dedicated time with God each day – on your own, with your family or with a friend? Note your own opinion and be ready to discuss it in the group.

We pray and read God's Word neither in order to earn a reward nor from fear of punishment. Rather, our motive is to come close to God and to grow spiritually strong.

And remember: we grow strong not just by reading or listening to God's Word, but even more by **obeying** it!

Come Follow Me

LESSON 6 PRACTICAL TASK

Start to spend a daily time with God, using the three steps you learned in questions 21-23. Find a good time and place for this and take at least 15 minutes each day. Start reading from the beginning of 1 Peter and read a few verses each day. Whatever God tells you through this, be ready to share with the group next week.

LESSON 6 REVIEW

1 Here are two followers of Christ:

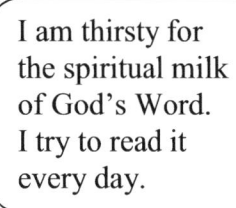

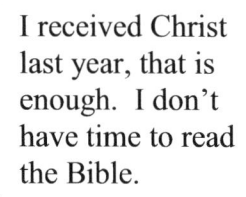

Adnan: "I am thirsty for the spiritual milk of God's Word. I try to read it every day."

Javed: "I received Christ last year, that is enough. I don't have time to read the Bible."

   a) Which of these two, Javed or Adnan, will grow spiritually strong? _____
   b) What happens to babies who are not thirsty for milk? _____

2 Why do we call the Bible the Word of God? Because: *(tick one)*
   ____ a) It speaks only about God and nothing else
   ____ b) The writers spoke from God as they were carried along by His Spirit
   ____ c) It is the copy of a book in heaven
   ____ d) It was dictated by the angel Gabriel

3 What are the two main sections of the Bible?
   The _____ Testament and the _____ Testament

4 It is good to spend a daily time with God. Write three suggested steps for how to spend this time:
   Step 1: _____
   Step 2: _____
   Step 3: _____

LESSON 6 ANSWERS

1. B
2. a) & b) your personal answers, before God
3. c)
4. Word
5. crave, milk, grow
6. prophets, God
7. a) False   b) True
8. God, Spirit
9. b)
10. a)
11. New
12. Old
13. b)
14. a) Old   b) New   c) continue
15. Praise be to
16. every day
17. c)
18. a) & b) for discussion time
19. a)
20. b)
21. Step 1: Prepare, Step 2: Read, Step 3: Pray
22. for discussion time

Study tip: Ask someone to pray regularly for you as you do this course.

Come Follow Me

Lesson 7 <u>Members of Christ's Church</u>

Suppose there is a new believer named Majid. Two years ago he started listening to radio programmes about Jesus Christ. The messages about forgiveness warmed his heart, and last year Majid took the step of commitment to become Jesus' follower. He did this in the privacy of his own house, by praying to God on his own.

Since then, Majid has never met with other followers of Christ. He is afraid to do so, in case his family found out. Also he says,

> I don't know if can trust the others in the meeting. Later they might betray me. It is safer if I keep my faith secret.

1	Do you think Majid is wise to keep his faith secret, or should he take the risk to join with a group of believers? Write your own opinion and be ready to share it in this week's discussion.

_____

2	In today's lesson we will study this matter. In your Bible, using the 'list of contents', find the first letter of Peter (1 Peter). Now turn to chapter 2, verse 4. How may we write this? (*tick one*)

　　___ a) 1 Peter 2:4　　___ b) 1 Peter 4:2　　___ c) 2 Peter 2:4

> 1 Peter chapter 2 gives at least three beautiful descriptions of Christ's church:
> 　　A) A spiritual house
> 　　B) A chosen people
> 　　C) A family
>
> If Majid could understand why Christ's community is so precious, maybe he will be more motivated to join it!

A) A Spiritual House

3	Now that you are using your own Bible, we will no longer write out all the verses for you. You can look them up for yourself. The instructions for this will be in this kind of box.

Read 1 Peter chapter 2 verses 4-5 and fill the blank spaces from verse 5:
"You also, like living stones, are being built into a _____ house".

Lesson Seven

4   A spiritual house is where God lives by his Spirit. It is not wrong to dedicate buildings for worship, but God does not need them to dwell in. He cares more about the 'spiritual house' of his people when they gather together in worship. <u>We</u> are God's house, <u>we</u> are God's church.

With what kind of stones does God want to build his spiritual house? (*tick one*):

    ___ a) ordinary stones, with which we build our own houses
    ___ b) 'living stones', i.e. Christ's followers

5   In verse 5 Christ's followers are described as 'living stones'. But a stone on its own is of little use. Even a pile of stones is useless, until a mason fits them together to make a house. God wants to fit together his people as 'living stones' to make a spiritual house.

So, which is more important for us: to build beautiful buildings for God or to meet together as his people? _____

6   The earliest followers of Christ did not have special buildings for worship. Perhaps they could not afford it, or perhaps it was too risky at times of persecution. So where did they hold their meetings? Read the following New Testament verses:

- "*Aquila and Priscilla greet you warmly in the Lord, and so does the church that meets at their house.*" (1 Corinthians 16:19)
- "*to Apphia our sister and Archippus our fellow soldier - and to the church that meets in your home.*" (Philemon 2)

So, in New Testament times, where did the churches usually meet to worship? (*tick one*):

    ___ a) in special church buildings
    ___ b) in the homes of their members
    ___ c) in mosques

7   Whenever we meet together as Christ's followers, even as a tiny group in our own homes, he dwells among us in a special way.

The Lord Jesus told his followers, "*Where two or three gather in my name, there am I with them*" (Matthew 18:20). Therefore what is the <u>minimum</u> number of believers needed for Christ to be present in this special way, by his Spirit? (*tick one*)

    ___ a) 100 believers   ___ b) 10 believers   ___ c) 2 or 3 believers

8   So if you know only one other person who loves Jesus Christ, don't worry! When you meet with that person to pray, who has promised to be present with you in a special way by his Spirit? _____

9   Have you sensed this special presence of Jesus Christ when you meet to worship with his followers? Write your own experience:

_____

10   But Majid at the beginning of this lesson refuses to meet with other believers. He is still Christ's follower, but is he actively part of the 'spiritual house' which God is building in his neighbourhood?   [Yes / No]

43

Come Follow Me

Let's come now to 1 Peter 2:9 for the next description of Christ's church.

B) A Chosen People

11   Read 1 Peter 2:9-10 and fill the blank spaces:

> "You are
> a _____ _____
> a royal priesthood,
> a holy nation,
> God's special possession,
> that you may declare the praises of him who called you
> out of darkness into his wonderful light."   (1 Peter 2:9)

Now memorize this verse, with its reference.

12   In this world, some nations consider themselves to be God's chosen race, superior to other nations. But who are called 'a chosen people' in 1 Peter 2:9? *(tick one)*
___ a) Arabs   ___ b) Jews   ___ c) Christ's followers

13   Yes, in Christ <u>we</u> are God's chosen people! Our master Jesus was '*rejected* by humans but *chosen* by God and *precious* to him' (1 Peter 2:4). We his followers are also rejected by humans; but who has chosen us and called us precious? _____

14   The Arabic translation of 1 Peter 2:9 says we are God's '*ummah*' (worldwide community of believers). Christ's followers from which of the following ethnic groups are included in His 'ummah'?   *(tick one or more correct answers)*

___ Pakistanis   ___ Arabs   ___ Iranians   ___ Turks   ___ Americans
___ Malays   ___ Chinese   ___ Jews   ___ Bangladeshis ___ Indonesians

15   What an amazing privilege we have to belong to this 'ummah'! It unites us in Christ from all our different backgrounds. You can taste this privilege whenever you meet Christ's follower from a different ethnic group than yourself, or when you belong to a local church with members of many backgrounds.

1 Peter 2:9 also explains God's purpose in making us his chosen people: "*that you may declare the praises of him who called you out of darkness into his wonderful light*".

For what purpose, then, has God chosen us?
___ a) so that we take pride in being better than other nations
___ b) so that we may declare his praises among the nations

16   Yes, God's chosen people must make him known among all tribes, ethnic groups and nations. He has called us out of darkness into his wonderful light. Now we must shine for him in the darkness!

Here are two followers of Christ in a country where the church is suppressed:

1 Whenever God brings to birth a group of Christ's followers in one city of our country, it is like a candle in the middle of darkness.

2 Yes, and just imagine if there were more such groups, light would increase throughout that city and spread to the towns and villages too!

3 But do you think that will really happen?

4 Yes, God can do it! But we must play our part too and shine like candles.

For what has God chosen us? To "_____ the _____ of him who called us out of darkness into his wonderful light".

17   Now write again the verse you memorized earlier (see question 11).

"You are
a _____
a royal priesthood,
a _____,
_____ special possession,
that you may _____ of him who called you
out of_____ into _____."   (1 Peter ___:9)

18   Revision   In 1 Peter chapter 2, which two descriptions of Christ's church have we studied so far? *(tick two)*
  ___ a) a spiritual house
  ___ b) a chosen people
  ___ c) a family

C) A Family

19   In lesson 3 we learned that all Christ's followers have the right to call God 'Father'. Therefore, as God's spiritual children, how are we related to each other?
  ___ a) as brothers and sisters   ___ b) merely as friends

Come Follow Me

20   Yes, through Jesus Christ you and I are members of the same spiritual family, with God as our heavenly Father. That makes us brothers and sisters to each other.

In 1 Peter 2:17, we are instructed to respect everyone but especially to love whom? 'The _____ of believers'.

21   When you were born, you had no choice about who are your physical brothers and sisters. Likewise, when you received new birth in Christ, you could not choose your spiritual brothers and sisters. You belong to them and they belong to you.

Who belongs to the family of believers? *(tick one)*
   ___ a) Anyone who has received new birth into God's family, through Christ
   ___ b) Anyone who is related to you by physical birth
   ___ c) Anyone who has joined your family through marriage

22   It is the same for us today. When we love Jesus Christ it breaks down the division between black and white, rich and poor, men and women, young and old! God's Word says,

> "So in Christ Jesus you are all children of God through faith... There is neither Jew nor Greek, slave nor free, nor is there male and female, for you are all one in Christ Jesus."
> (Galatians 3:26-28)

Our family in Christ overcomes all our other differences. We are 'all one in Christ Jesus'. Circle 'Yes' or No' for the following questions:

a) Should Christ's followers from different ethnic groups be willing to eat together? [Yes / No]
b) Should a doctor and a street cleaner be willing to worship together if they both love Jesus? [Yes / No]

What about you?
- *Which ethnic or social groups would you normally not associate with at all?*
- *If someone from that group becomes Christ's follower, will this break down the barrier enough for you to have fellowship with him/her?*

Be ready for discussion.

> 1 Peter chapter 2 describes Christ's followers as a 'spiritual house', a 'chosen people' and a 'family'. Also, 1 Peter chapter 4 calls us 'Christians'. But, surprisingly, this word 'Christian' hardly comes at all in the Bible! So we are free to describe ourselves with different terms, if we wish.
>
> Some people in our society have a wrong understanding of what 'Christian' means. For this reason, would we perhaps be wiser to call ourselves 'followers of Christ'? Let's discuss this in the discussion time.

Do You need Christ's Church?
23   Think of many pieces of charcoal burning red-hot on a barbecue stall.
a) While all the pieces remain in the fire, do they stay hot or cold? _____
b) But if you push one piece of charcoal out of the fire and leave it on the side, what will happen to it? _____

24   Our spiritual lives are like the pieces of charcoal. Remaining in the warmth of fellowship with other believers, we are like the charcoal which stays hot in the fire. But if we cut ourselves off from Christ's church, what will happen to our faith?
_____

25   Are you regularly meeting with other followers of Christ? If not, why not?
_____

Prayer

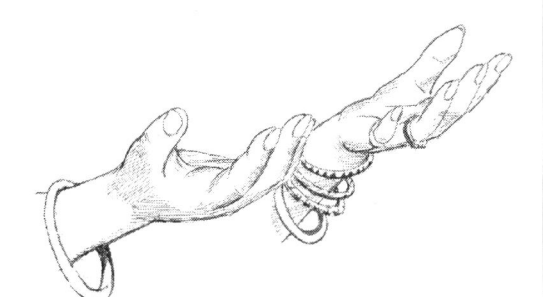

"Father God,
Thank you for other believers who help me keep warm like the charcoal in the fire.
Help me to play my part actively in Christ's church.
Thank you for making me part of your chosen people.
Amen"

LESSON 7 PRACTICAL TASK

Hopefully you are already part of a local group of believers. Make sure that you meet with them this week. If you are not yet able to join a group publicly, at least meet up with one other follower of Christ this week.

LESSON 7 REVIEW

1   What three descriptions of Christ's church have we learned according to the teaching of 1 Peter chapter 2?
  a) a spiritual _____
  b) a _____ people
  c) a _____

2   When two or three believers meet to pray and worship, who is present in a special way with them? _____ *(see question 9)*

3   Write again the memory verse.

"You are
a _____,
a _____,
a _____,
_____,
that you may _____ of him who _____
_____." (1 Peter __ : __)

Come Follow Me

LESSON 7 ANSWERS

1. for discussion
2. a)
3. spiritual
4. b)
5. meet together as his people
6. b)
7. c)
8. Jesus Christ
9. personal response
10. No
11. chosen people
12. c)
13. God
14. all the answers are correct
15. b)
16. declare, praises
17. check with the verse in question 11
18. a), b)
19. a)
20. family
21. a)
22. a) Yes b) Yes
23. a) hot b) it will grow cold
24. it will grow cold
25. personal answer (if you wish, discuss this with your advisor privately)

Study tip: Are you doing the practical tasks for each lesson? Is this bringing change in your life?

Lesson 8 Members of Two Communities

It is commonly thought that people who change their religion have betrayed their family and community. But does changing our personal faith really make us traitors? Don't we still love our people?

> In this lesson we will learn how we can try to be loyal to our family and community as well as being loyal to our Saviour Jesus.

Members of Two Communities

1   Our permanent homeland is with Christ forever. In this world, as 1 Peter 2:11 says, we are 'foreigners and exiles' (or 'aliens and strangers' in another translation).

a) Where are we temporary residents?   [in this world / with Christ forever] *(circle one)*
b) Where are we permanent citizens?   [in this world / with Christ forever]

2   For the period of our lives on this earth, God has a good purpose for us to fulfil here. Thus we are members of two communities at the same time. We belong to our <u>spiritual community</u>, which is Christ's church, and at the same time to our <u>earthly community</u> which is the society in which we were born.

So, which <u>one</u> of the following statements is true?
___ a) We belong only in our earthly community
___ b) We belong only in our spiritual community
___ c) We belong in both communities at the same time

3   Was it by mistake that you were born into a particular society and nation? No, this was God's wise plan. He decided the place and time of your birth. Or maybe you have migrated to another country where you now are trying to settle. Don't worry, your Father God knows about that too. He wants you to be gladly a member of two communities. What are they? *(write 'earthly' or 'spiritual' in the correct places:)*

a) Our _____ community, which is the society where we live
b) Our _____ community, which is Christ's church

4   But often, even when we want to play a positive role in our earthly community, other people are negative towards us. They view us with suspicion.

At the time 1 Peter was written, Christ's followers faced the same difficulty. Non-Christians accused them of 'doing wrong' (1 Peter 2:12).

Come Follow Me

a) Do you think those believers found it easy or hard to hear such untrue slander? _____

b) Have you faced any similar experience of people making false accusations against you? Write about it here. _____
_____

Doing Good

5 It is always hard to bear false accusations from people. They call us 'infidel' (*kafir*) and 'apostate' (*murtadd*) even though we believe in God. They call us traitors even though we are loyal to our people! How should we respond to our accusers?

By our words alone, it is difficult to convince them. But instead, says 1 Peter 2:15, "it is God's will that by _____ _____ you should silence the ignorant talk of foolish people" *(read the verse and fill the blanks)*.

6 Here is a true story:

> In a certain country of North Africa, Christ's church is growing. In one town there, the local religious leaders became angry about this growth. They complained to the town mayor that "you should arrest these traitors". "No, I won't arrest them", replied the mayor. "Since their group started to grow in this town, the crime rate has gone down".

So, what is the best way to defend ourselves when people accuse us falsely? *(tick one)*
  ___ a) by complaining
  ___ b) by doing good
  ___ c) by fighting back

7 By 'doing good', we prove that we love our nation, our culture, our language, our society, our tribe and our family group. In your opinion, which of the following will be good ways to do this? *(tick more than one)*
  ___ a) We should pray for our nation and for its leaders
  ___ b) We should serve our neighbourhood wherever we live
  ___ c) We should long to emigrate to another country as soon as possible
  ___ d) We should appreciate our local poetry and music
  ___ e) We should work for the uplift of our village or local community
  ___ f) We should refuse to attend the funeral of our non-Christian relatives
  ___ g) We should contribute to the wedding expenses of our non-Christian cousins

8 Our Lord looks with compassion on our nation. He wants to build up our earthly community, to give it a better future. Whom can he use for this great purpose? Us, who are 'God's chosen people' in this land!

In which ways may God want to use you as a channel of blessing to your relatives and your community? *(note your ideas and be ready to share them in the group)*
_____

9 In which two communities has God placed us?
  a) in Christ's _____ which is our spiritual community
  b) in our society which is our _____ community

Lesson Eight

Submitting to our Government

10   The early Christians endured not only slander from the general public, but also persecution from the Roman government. The Roman rulers thought:

> We must clamp down on these Christians! They call Jesus Christ their king, so they are traitors against the king of Rome.

The Roman emperor Nero persecuted and even tortured Christ's followers. He enjoyed feeding them alive to the lions, or covering them with oil and setting them on fire!

How did the apostle Peter tell his readers to respond to such an unfair king and government? Read 1 Peter 2:13-14 and tick the correct answer:
   ___ a) fight back with weapons
   ___ b) submit, for the Lord's sake
   ___ c) deny they were followers of Jesus

11   According to 1 Peter 2:13, what attitude should we show towards the government authorities? We should 's_____, for the Lord's sake'.

12   Christ's followers are not rebels. We do not overthrow our governments. But what if our rulers tell us to do something against God? Should we obey them then?

One time the religious rulers commanded the apostle Peter to stop teaching the people about Jesus Christ. But Peter replied bravely, *"We must obey God rather than human beings!"* (Acts 5:29). So the rulers whipped him and he submitted to this punishment.

a) Did Peter <u>obey</u> the rulers on this occasion?   [Yes / No]
b) Did he still <u>submit</u> to their punishment, for the Lord's sake?   [Yes / No]

13   What should we do if the government oppresses the people? Should we just submit quietly or protest against it?

Or what if the authorities ban us from meeting together as believers, or reading the Bible, or teaching our children about Jesus Christ? What should we do then? Note your ideas and be ready for discussion:

_____
_____
_____

Come Follow Me

Submitting to our Boss

14   Read 1 Peter 2:18 To whom is this verse written? *(tick one)*
      ___ a) husbands   ___ b) wives   ___ c) slaves

15   Just think:
   - It is easy to submit to a boss who is 'good and considerate', but 1 Peter 2:18 tells us to submit even to those who are 'harsh'.
   - It is easy to work for high wages, but the slaves in 1 Peter 2:18 worked for no wages at all! They were the property of their masters and had to obey them in everything.

Even then, what were the slaves told to do? "Iin reverent fear of God _____ yourselves to your masters".

16   Are you working on low wages for a harsh boss? Even in these unfair circumstances, what should our attitude be, according to 1 Peter 2:18? *(tick one)*
      ___ a) do as little work as possible
      ___ b) feel bitter resentment in our hearts
      ___ c) submit ourselves to our boss with all respect
      ___ d) complain to everyone about our harsh boss

17   <u>My true story</u> I used to work in a factory under a manager who never showed appreciation for my hard work. Yet one time I made a small mistake. In fact, it wasn't even my mistake, it was the fault of a worker under me. Yet my boss blamed me and gave me a written warning! That day I had to fight hard in my heart against resentment. Can you guess what verse from God's Word helped me gain the victory? Yes, it was 1 Peter 2:18!

Now, let's think about another aspect of our work. Place a tick on any of the following professions which you think are 'noble' or 'honourable':
___ shepherd   ___ doctor   ___ government minister   ___ fisherman
___ engineer   ___ carpenter   ___ university lecturer   ___ tailor

18   Perhaps you wrote that 'doctor, government minister, engineer or university lecturer' are the honourable ones. Perhaps you are not ambitious for your son to become a 'shepherd, fisherman, carpenter or tailor'. But did you know that some of the most honourable people of the Bible did ordinary manual jobs?

Match these people with their professions:

People	Professions
a) prophet David	carpenter
b) Jesus the Messiah	fisherman
c) the apostle Peter	tailor (making tents)
d) the apostle Paul	shepherd

(If you don't know all the answers, check them at the end of this lesson)

19   Even though all these four people were honourable spiritual leaders, yet they felt no shame to work with their hands.

So, which of the following workers has more honour in God's sight? *(tick one)*

___ a) a trash collector who does his work well, for the Lord's sake

___ b) a university lecturer who sells grades for a bribe

20   Some people, when they become Christ's followers, are thrown out of their good jobs. They have to find any work they can, in order to survive. In India, a person became Christ's follower from the same previous religion as you. He describes what happened next:

> "My father became furious. He grabbed a large stick and began to beat me. He beat me so hard that the stick broke in half. I was compelled to leave home.
>
> Everywhere I went, I inquired about a job – but to no avail. While I was waiting, an army officer asked me to be his servant. It was a menial job. I had come from a prominent family, in fact I had had my own servant. I was being asked to become someone else's personal servant! I rebelled against the very idea. I was hungry, but it seemed better to starve than to lower myself to that extent.
>
> In the inner struggle I experienced, I knew that God was teaching me a very important lesson. The Lord Jesus said that he did not come to be served but to serve. I, too, had to experience the meaning of serving in humility. God gave me the willingness and courage to accept the job. God enabled me to be a loyal and efficient servant."
>
> *(from 'The Truth Path' by Mark Hanna)*

1 Peter 2 tells us we should have the same attitude to our boss as to the government. What is it? ' S_____ '

Summary
21   Remember, we belong to two communities at the same time.
   In the words of 1 Peter 2:17,
   - We "show proper respect to everyone" - as members of our society and nation
   - We "love the family of believers" - as members of Christ's church.

We have responsibilities towards both communities. For each of the responsibilities below, write 'earthly' or 'spiritual' according to which community it relates to *(the first one has been done for you)*.

Come Follow Me

Our responsibility	Which community?
a) We try to be the best citizens of our nation	_earthly_
b) We meet regularly with our brothers and sisters in Christ	_____
c) We submit to our government and pray for our rulers	_____
d) We submit to our boss and work hard for him or her	_____
e) We build each other up in our Christian faith	_____

22   To remind yourself of these twofold responsibilities, memorize 1 Peter 2:17 now:

> "Show proper respect to everyone, love the family of believers"   (1 Peter 2:17)

And let's try to be loyal to both communities!

LESSON 8 PRACTICAL TASK

During the next week,

- do one of the things that you wrote in point 7 or 8

or

- do something to help a needy person

or

- do something extra for your non-Christian boss (at work or at home) that you would not normally do

---

LESSON 8 REVIEW

1   Of which two communities are we members?

    a) Our _____ community which is Christ's church
    b) Our _____ community which is our society and nation

2   What one word summarizes the attitude we should have to the government and also to our boss? _____

3   Write the memory verse here:
    " _____ "
    (1 Peter ___ : ___)

LESSON 8 ANSWERS

1. a) in this world   b) with Christ forever
2. c)
3. a) earthly   b) spiritual
4. a) I am sure you wrote 'hard'
   b) your personal answer
5. doing good
6. b)
7. share your answers in discussion
8. be ready to share your ideas
9. a) church   b) earthly
10. b)
11. submit
12. a) No   b) Yes
13. for discussion
14. c)
15. submit
16. c)
17. your personal answer
18. a) shepherd (see 1 Samuel 17:15)
    b) carpenter (see Mark 6:3)
    c) fisherman (see Mark 1:16)
    d) tailor (see Acts 18:3)
19. a)
20. submit
21. a) earthly   b) spiritual   c) earthly   d) earthly   e) spiritual
22. memorize the verse

Study tip: Whenever a question says "give your own experience", *write* your answer and be ready for discussion.

Lesson 9 Reasons for Persecution

If your relatives and friends know about your decision to follow Jesus Christ, they are probably very angry with you. Or perhaps it is still a secret, but you fear what they will do when they find out.

Do not be surprised at this opposition! Sometimes following Christ is like walking on a path of thorns. No-one likes to suffer. However, our master Jesus has trod this thorny path first himself. With him at our side we will find it is also a path of joy and the path to glory.

The Christian life: path of thorns, path of flowers

Today we will learn four reasons why Christ's followers are persecuted.

First Reason: The World Hates Us

1   Our Lord Jesus said to his disciples, *"you do not belong to the world, but I have chosen you out of the world. That is why the world hates you"*. (John 15:19)

Therefore, as Christ's followers what do we expect to receive from non-Christians around us?
   ___ a) persecution   ___ b) love   *(tick one)*

2   We are 'God's chosen people' but the world will hate us. In what ways, until now, have you faced opposition for being Jesus Christ's follower?
(tick one or more answers, according to your own experience)
   ___ a) Your friends mocked you and turned away from you
   ___ b) Your relatives cut off contact with you
   ___ c) You were physically beaten
   ___ d) You were forced to leave home
   ___ e) Someone threatened to kill you
   ___ f) You lost your job
   ___ g) People have not persecuted you too much
   ___ h) You have not yet suffered because your faith in Christ is still secret
   ___ i) Any other experience of persecution:_____

3   We can suffer in different ways. One believer told me, "I could endure the beatings from my father, but the tears of my mother were much harder to bear!"

Another form of persecution is when our relatives try to snatch our land or other property. There is certainly a risk of losing our earthly 'inheritance' in this way. But according to 1 Peter 1:4, we have another "_____ *that can never perish, spoil or fade. This inheritance is kept in heaven for you*". Read 1 Peter 1:4 and fill the blank space.

4   So even if we lose our temporary property for Christ's sake let's take courage, because we will receive an eternal inheritance instead.

a) Which kind of inheritance will 'perish, spoil or fade': earthly inheritance or heavenly?
_____

b) Which kind of inheritance can never 'perish, spoil or fade': earthly inheritance or heavenly?
_____

5   It feels very hard to lose our inheritance on this earth, but our inheritance in paradise is much greater.

> In the 1970's the government of Cambodia was persecuting Christ's followers. A believer named Haim was arrested with his whole family. They were forced to dig a large grave-hole. Haim, with his wife and children knelt in prayer by the grave. He comforted them with these words, "We are gathered for a short while here by this grave, but will soon be around God's throne, free forever in paradise."
>
> As the victims' bodies fell down into the pit, their souls soared up to the place their heavenly Father had prepared for them.
>
> *(from 'Killing Fields, Living Fields' by Don Cormack)*

What did Haim and his family gain? *(tick one)*
    ___ a) a long life on this earth   ___ b) an eternal inheritance

So in Christ, even if we die, we still gain life!

6   What is the first reason we are persecuted? Because the world _____ us.

Second Reason: God Allows Persecution

7   Read 1 Peter 1:5. Whose power shields us during our lives on earth? _____'s power.

8   God's power is like a shield protecting us. It is important for us to understand that:
- *God is all-powerful*. Therefore everything he allows us to face, including persecution, is under his control.
- *God is all-loving*. Therefore everything he allows us to endure, even persecution, is for our good.

We are God's chosen people. Who allows persecution, for our good? _____

Come Follow Me

9   Because God our Father loves us so much, He disciplines us. He deliberately allows us to pass through hard trials. Read 1 Peter 1:6-7

According to verse 7,
   a) What does the goldsmith use to purify gold?_____
   b) What does God our Father use to purify our faith? _____

10   God our Father allows 'all kinds of trials' to purify our faith just as fire purifies gold.

Imtiaz was severely persecuted when he became Christ's follower. Later he studied for three years at Bible college. But he said, "college is not what made me strong – persecution did".

In the school of suffering, God our Father trains us to become patient, trusting, loving and obedient. Our 'older brother' Jesus Christ was trained in the same way.

Why do you think God allows you to suffer? *(tick one or more according to your opinion)*
   ___ a) for your own good
   ___ b) because he doesn't care about you
   ___ c) because he likes to hurt you
   ___ d) because he is not strong enough to stop your suffering

11   The book of Romans, chapter 8 gives us strength to face suffering. It says

"We know that in all things God works for the good of those who love him, who have been called according to his purpose."   (Romans 8:28)

a) According to this verse, will God work for our good even through hard times? _____

b) Think back to a hard time you faced as Christ's follower. How did he work for good in it, and what did he teach you? *(note your ideas and be ready to share them in discussion)*
_____
_____

12   Romans chapter 8 continues with another wonderful promise:

"If God is for us, who can be against us?...Who shall separate us from the love of Christ? Shall trouble or hardship or persecution or famine or nakedness or danger or sword?... No, in all these things we are more than conquerors through him who loved us".   (Romans 8:35-37)

Can even death separate us from Christ's love?   [Yes / No]

13   Till now, what two reasons have we learned for why we face persecution?
   First reason: The world _____ us   *(questions 1-7)*
   Second reason: _____ allows persecution   *(questions 8-13)*

Here is a third reason we can be persecuted:

Third Reason: We sometimes Act Foolishly

14   Not all persecution is necessary or beneficial. Sometimes we bring unnecessary suffering on ourselves by our foolish behaviour. Read the following true story:

A young man named Shakeel lived in a town in Pakistan. His father was a shrine-guardian so Shakeel's family was highly respected in the neighbourhood. But at the age of 20, while travelling in a distant city, Shakeel experienced healing in Jesus' name and became his follower.

> Later he returned to his own non-Christian family and told them about his decision. They were worried that, because of Shakeel, they would lose their reputation and their income from the shrine. But Shakeel did not care about this and he made his new faith public. This brought embarrassment to the family. When the opposition from his father increased, Shakeel ran away to a big city. Later he wrote a letter to his father, angrily accusing him that "you do not financially support me and you no longer love me."
>
> After some time Shakeel returned home. His mother was willing to accept him, but his father said, "You insulted me in writing. Now I will not accept you back".

In your opinion, in what ways did Shakeel act foolishly? Write your ideas and be ready for discussion.

_____
_____
_____

15   So let's learn to distinguish between 'necessary' persecution and 'unnecessary' persecution.
- *Necessary persecution* is what Christ's followers face for being loyal to him;
- *Unnecessary persecution* takes place if Christ's followers behave in foolish or disrespectful ways towards non-Christians.

a) 1 Peter 2:19 says, *"It is commendable if someone bears up under the pain of unjust suffering because they are conscious of God."* Is this 'necessary' or 'unnecessary' persecution?

_____

b) 1 Peter 2:20 continues, *"But how is it to your credit if you receive a beating for doing wrong and endure it?"* Is this 'necessary' or 'unnecessary' persecution? _____

16   Our decision to follow Christ was the correct one. But maybe it caused our dear family members to suffer. Our parents may feel pain that we rejected the path in which they trained us. Our sisters may find it harder to find a good marriage arrangement because of our reputation. Our relatives may feel we dishonoured the family name.

So let us remain loyal to our Lord, but also try to avoid causing unnecessary shame for our families.

Stop and think:
> *Are you doing anything to cause unnecessary shame for your non-Christian relatives? Or unnecessary persecution for yourself?*

17   If opposition increases in our home community, we should be wise. Sometimes the wisest action is to escape to another place, sometimes it is better to stay and endure the opposition. In the book of Acts, on some occasions Christ's followers fled from danger, on other occasions they remained.

In what circumstances would you advise someone to run away from persecution? Note your ideas and be ready for discussion _____
_____

1 Peter gives us a fourth reason we will surely face persecution.

Come Follow Me

Fourth Reason: We Follow in Christ's Steps

18 *"A servant is not greater than his master"*, Christ reminded his followers, *"If they persecuted me, they will persecute you also"*. (John 15:20).

Whose steps do we follow when we are persecuted? _____'s steps.

19   Read 1 Peter 2:21-25.

a) Did Jesus deserve to suffer? *(see verse 22)*   [Yes / No]
b) How did he react to his unjust punishment? *(read verse 23 and tick one)*
    ___ 1. he cursed his enemies
    ___ 2. he defended himself
    ___ 3. he entrusted himself to God

20   Our beloved Christ trod the 'path of thorns', all the way to his death. He suffered insults and whippings. The crowds shouted for his death. His closest friends ran away. Then the Roman soldiers nailed him to a cross; they used this agonizing form of torture for the worst kind of criminals.

Why was the honourable Son of God willing to suffer this worst form of pain and dishonour? 1 Peter 2:24 gives the answer: *"He himself bore our _____ in his body on the cross"*.

21   We deserved to die. Instead, Christ died for our sake and in our place. *"By his wounds you have been healed"* (verse 24). In all the world there is no greater example of love than this!

> ➢ *Pause now to thank the Lord Jesus for loving you enough to give his life for you. You may use this prayer:*

"Dear Lord Jesus,
Thank you for bearing so much pain and shame on the cross, for me.
I know that as your follower I too will bear pain and shame.
Help me to follow in your steps.
Amen"

22   When we become Jesus' followers, we are not just changing a religion, getting baptized, praising the Lord and enjoying his sweet presence. No, we must also follow in Christ's steps, even if that includes suffering.

Memorize this verse, together with its reference.

"Christ suffered for you, leaving you an example, that you should follow in his steps"
(1 Peter 2:21)

Summary

23   From 1 Peter chapters 1 and 2 we have learned four reasons why Christ's followers face persecution:

    first reason: The world hates us
    second reason: God allows persecution
    third reason: We sometimes act foolishly
    fourth reason: We follow in _____'s steps *(fill the blank)*

LESSON 9 PRACTICAL TASK

In today's lesson there are many comforting verses from the Holy Bible. Each day this week, look at a different verse from this lesson and think what it means in your life. You will find these verses in points 1, 3, 7, 9, 11, 15, 18, 20 and 22 of today's lesson.

LESSON 9 REVIEW

1 Write the memory verse, together with its reference.
"Christ suffered _____
_____" (1 Peter ___ : ___)

2 What four reasons have we learned, about why Christ's followers face persecution?
first reason: The _____ _____ us
second reason: _____ allows _____
third reason: We sometimes _____ _____
fourth reason: We follow in _____'s _____

LESSON 9 ANSWERS

1. a)
2. personal response
3. inheritance
4. a) earthly   b) heavenly
5. b)
6. hates
7. God's
8. God
9. a) fire   b) all kinds of trials
10. for the discussion time
11. a) yes   b) for discussion
12. No
13. hates, God
14. for discussion
15. a) necessary   b) unnecessary
16. stop and think
17. for discussion
18. Christ
19. a) No   b) 3
20. sins
21. pause to pray
22. memorize the verse
23. Christ

Study tip: Are you following all three parts of the course method? Look again at the picture on page iv.

Lesson 10 Reacting to Persecution

Here two followers of Christ are talking about how they react to insults and persecution:

When someone insults me, my blood boils. I would rather die than to be insulted. How can I forget when another person has stabbed me so deep, like a dagger into my heart?

Me too. When someone hurts me I want to hurt him back. Honour demands I must take revenge. It's a sign of weakness just to forgive. Christ tells me to forgive my enemy, but it is very hard...

So, what do you think? When people persecute us, how should we react? 1 Peter chapters 3 and 4 will help us answer this question.

The Cycle of Revenge

1   When someone insults or hurts us, don't we want to hurt him or her in return? Taking revenge is our natural human reaction. Which of the following proverbs expresses this idea? *(tick one)*

    ___ a) 'An eye for an eye'
    ___ b) 'Turn the other cheek'

2   Taking revenge is our way to keep our honour. But when someone hurts us and we strike back, it does not stop there. That person will react worse in turn. This leads to a cycle of revenge. It goes round and round like this:

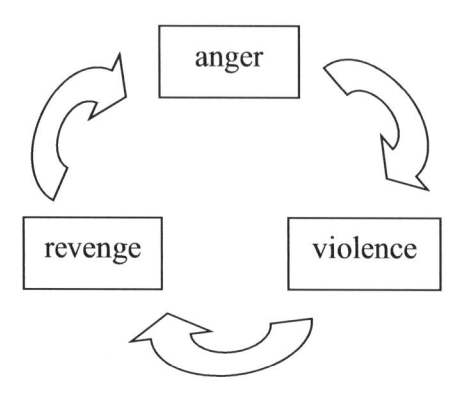

anger → violence → revenge → (anger)

Can you think of an example where you have seen this cycle of revenge getting worse and worse? Note it here and be ready for discussion. _____

3   Think about the news on our televisions. How many nations have been torn apart by anger, violence and revenge! Revenge brings a curse on nations. How can this curse be broken? How can this cycle of revenge be stopped?

> ➤ *Stop and think about a nation you love. Ask God to set it free from the cycle of revenge.*

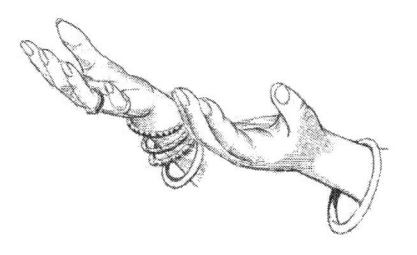

Forgiveness instead of Revenge

4   Jesus Christ taught us how to break free from the cycle of revenge. He said

| "Love your enemies and pray for those who persecute you"   (Matthew 5:44) |

Write this command here again, and memorize it:
"Love _____" (_____ 5:44)

5   It is very difficult to forgive our enemies! But Jesus Christ did not merely teach this, he put it into practice. As Roman soldiers hammered sharp spikes into his hands and feet, he prayed *"Father, forgive them, for they do not know what they are doing"*! (Luke 23:34)

Many great leaders ended their lives on the battlefield, cursing their enemies. By contrast, how did our Lord Jesus end his life?   *(tick one)*
    ___ a) with forgiveness   ___ b) with revenge

6   Do you remember the memory verse from the last lesson? Fill the blanks: *"Christ suffered for you, leaving you an example, that you should _____ in his _____"* (1 Peter 2:___)

7   We should 'follow in his steps'. Therefore, when we are insulted or persecuted, what should be our reaction?
    ___ a) revenge   ___ b) forgiveness

8   Many people think that we are strong if we take revenge, and weak if we forgive others or endure their insults. But Jesus Christ showed us the opposite. According to his example, what is true Christian 'manliness': to take revenge, or to forgive? _____

9   Read this true story of a follower of Jesus in the Middle East, called Farid. Here he describes what happened one day, at the company where he worked:

> "Each person had their own locker, where he could store his tools and clothes. One time at the end of the month, I put my wages in my locker but I forgot to take them home with me at the end of the shift. The next day, I discovered that someone had broken into my locker and stolen the money.
>
> I wanted revenge! I suspected that one of my workmates had stolen the money, so I decided to break open their lockers and burn the contents. I grabbed a hammer, and prepared to strike - but suddenly felt as though an invisible hand grabbed my wrist, holding me back. Then I heard a gentle voice, saying: 'Don't avenge yourself. Don't give in to Satan.' "
>
> "I replied to the voice, 'Please put out the flames of my anger. Tell me what to do.'

When the 'flames of anger' are burning in our heart, we have to take the choice between revenge and forgiveness.

a) Which is like petrol on a fire, revenge or forgiveness? _____
b) Which is like water on a fire, revenge or forgiveness? _____

10   God's voice told Farid to write a letter forgiving the thief. Farid left the letter in the locker and went home full of joy. His account continues:

> "When I arrived in the office the next day, one of my colleagues was waiting for me. With a trembling voice, he said 'I was the one who broke your locker open. I found your letter yesterday, and was very moved. Where did you learn to act like that?'
>
> 'I'll tell you some other time,' I replied. But he kept asking, so I finally gave him a New Testament. One month later, he was ready to follow Jesus."
>
> *(a true account from the internet)*

Farid stopped the cycle of revenge. He absorbed the harm on himself.

a) Who urged Farid not to take revenge? _____
b) What was the result in the other man's life? _____
c) Think about someone who insulted or harmed you. Are you still planning revenge on that person? _____ *(your personal response)*

11   Instead of taking revenge, Farid forgave and blessed the person who hurt him. Read 1 Peter 3:9 and fill the blank spaces: *"Do not repay _____ with evil or _____ with insult. On the contrary repay evil with blessing".*

Come Follow Me

12   Miriam is a believer in Pakistan. Her true story is similar to Farid's, but the outcome was harder:

> Miriam was looking after the shared cash for the women in her neighbourhood. She had 15,000 rupees locked in a box. One time a neighbour came to get her money. Miriam gave her 5,000 rupees, then she put the box away. At that time her husband's aunt was visiting and saw everything. That afternoon the aunt went back home. The next day Miriam went to the box and noticed she hadn't locked it, and the money was gone. The aunt had stolen the 10,000 rupees!
>
> Miriam had to work for months to replace the money that was stolen, feeding her own children less. She was so angry with her relative. She even had difficulty praying. But one day, she realized how much she hated her aunt and she chose to forgive her. When she did, joy filled her heart and she was set free from her hate.

How did Miriam react to the person who caused her such a great loss? *(tick one)*
 ___ a) with revenge   ___ b) with forgiveness

13   When someone has harmed us, do you think we should always just keep quiet about it as Miriam did? Write your opinion and be ready for discussion:
_____

14   Sometimes it may be appropriate to protest when someone harms us, sometimes not. But in every case we still should forgive the person in our hearts. If we do not forgive, then the desire for revenge will rule our lives. Resentment will destroy our mental, physical and spiritual health, like an acid that destroys its own container. As a wise Afghan poet wrote:
 "Storing up grudges leads to discomfort
 Your heart hardens,
 In the end it brings a scorpion's sting."

To be set free from this 'scorpion's sting', what must we do about our persecutors?
_____ them.

15   One believer from Africa said,

> "I found it very hard to forgive those who beat me and left scars on my body. I wanted to pray they would go to hell. I felt like this for two years until God changed my attitude. Almost as much as I suffered from the persecution, I suffered afterwards through not forgiving my persecutors."

Bring to your mind the memory verse from question 4 and fill the blanks:
"Love _____ and pray for _____" (Matthew 5:44).

> In the above sentence, if the name of your enemies were written in the blank spaces, would you be able to forgive them? At the end of this lesson we will learn practical steps of forgiveness.

16   Our human instinct is to take revenge. But as God's chosen people, we need not be controlled by our human nature. We also have a 'new nature', which is Christ in us and us in him.   Circle 'Yes' or 'No' below:

a) In my old human nature, is it possible for me to forgive my persecutors?   [Yes / No]
b) Being in Christ, is it possible for me to forgive my persecutors?   [Yes / No]

Joy in our Sufferings
17   Read 1 Peter 4:12-13 and fill the blank spaces from verse 13 :
"But _____ inasmuch as you participate in the sufferings of Christ, so that you may be _____ when his glory is revealed".

18   We can 'rejoice' now even in our sufferings, and later we will be 'overjoyed' when we see our beloved Jesus in all his glory.

   Now read 1 Peter 4:14-16.

a) Which verse says we should not be ashamed to suffer as a Christian?   verse ____
b) Which verse says those who are insulted because of Christ's name are blessed? verse ____

19   Perhaps you have been deeply hurt by people's insults and lies. Perhaps even your closest family members have rejected you. Our loving Lord knows your pain. He will bind up your emotional wounds. And he gives you this promise:

> "Blessed are you when people insult you, persecute you and falsely say all kinds of evil against you because of me. Rejoice and be glad, because great is your reward in heaven"
> (Matthew 5:11-12)

In the box above, underline the words 'blessed', 'rejoice' and 'be glad'.

Summary
20   The way for Christ's followers to survive in this world that persecutes them, is to be like Christ himself! What two reactions to persecution have we learned in today's lesson?
   1. From 1 Peter chapter 3, _____ instead of Revenge *(questions 4-16)*
   2. From 1 Peter chapter 4, _____ in our Sufferings *(questions 17-19)*

LESSON 10 PRACTICAL TASK

In question 10c) of this lesson, you thought about a person who insulted or hurt you. Your task is to forgive that person from your heart. Go through the following steps:

Step 1): If you find it hard to forgive that person, think of Jesus Christ, who forgave his murderers as they hammered nails into his hands and feet. He forgave your sins too.

Step 2): If you are willing, decide to forgive that person. This is your choice. Not even God will force you to forgive. But if you don't forgive, then the anger will continue to burn inside you like an acid. The only way to find peace is to forgive.

Step 3): Pray this prayer:

"Dear Father God,
Help me to forgive XX [think of a person's name here but don't write it]
even though he/she hurt me.
I decide now to forgive him/her.
I can't do this in my own strength, but through the strength of Jesus Christ in me.
Please gradually heal my emotions of anger and revenge.
Amen."

Step 4): Remember, your decision to forgive comes first. Only later will you feel less angry towards that person. Keep praying until God takes away your anger. If this takes a long time, talk with another believer about it. You need not mention the person's name who hurt you.

These steps will help you forgive that person from your heart. This decision has set you free from the prison of revenge. However, your relationship with that person may still need to be restored. We will learn more about this in Lesson 12.

LESSON 10 REVIEW

1. We should 'follow in Christ's steps'. Therefore, when we are insulted or persecuted, what should be our reaction: revenge or forgiveness? _____

2. Write again the verse you memorized:
   "Love _____" (_____ 5:44)

LESSON 10 ANSWERS

1. a)
2. for discussion
3. stop and pray
4. memorize the verse
5. a)
6. check this yourself from lesson 9
7. b)
8. forgive
9. a) revenge b) forgiveness
10. a) God (through the voice)
    b) He later followed Jesus
    c) personal response
11. evil, insult
12. b)
13. for discussion
14. forgive
15. check the memory verse from question 4
16. a) No, b) Yes
17. read verse 13
18. a) verse 16 b) verse 14
19. underline the words
20. a) forgiveness, b) joy

Lesson 11   <u>Husbands and Wives</u>

The stories of Mullah Nasruddin are widely enjoyed in the Middle East and Asia.

In one story people asked Mullah Nasruddin, "When did your first marriage take place?" He answered, "I can't remember – but it was just before I got wise"!

We like to make jokes about marriage. But remember, your wife or husband is God's precious gift to you. And if you are not yet married, one day you may be, so this lesson will benefit you too!

God's Design for Marriage

1   Genesis, in the *Tawrat* (Books of Moses) gives very important teaching about marriage. As you know, Adam was created first. At this time Adam had no lack of servants, for the animals were there to obey him. But he lacked a companion, to be his closest friend.

God saw that *"it is not good for the man to be alone"*. (Genesis 2:18). So he created Eve to be Adam's wife. What did God make Eve to be? *(tick one)*
    ___ a) Adam's servant   ___ b) Adam's companion and friend

2   According to Genesis 1:27, Eve equally with Adam was created in God's image and likeness. They had equal value in God's sight.

This has important lessons for us today. Circle 'True' or 'False' by the following statements:

a) Men and women are of equal value in God's sight   [True / False]
b) Men are the peak of God's creatures and women are inferior   [True / False]
c) God created wives as servants to their husbands   [True / False]
d) God created wives as helpers and companions to their husbands   [True / False]

3   Our wise Creator gave Adam and Eve to each other in marriage. God's design for marriage is <u>one</u> man united with <u>one</u> woman, for their <u>whole</u> life.

> "That is why a man leaves his father and mother and is united to his wife, and they become one flesh".   (Genesis 2:24)

a) Whom should a man 'leave' when he gets married? His father and _____
b) With whom is he united, as 'one flesh'? His _____

4   In some countries it is not always possible for the husband physically to leave his parents' home as soon as he gets married. But emotionally, he should definitely 'leave' his father and mother and 'be united' to his bride. A man's unity with his wife is more important than his unity with his parents! (Of course, the new wife should also make an effort to fit in with her mother-in-law, and her husband can help in this).

According to Genesis 2:24, to whom should a man give first place in his love and loyalty?
  ___ a) his wife
  ___ b) his mother and father

5 Look at this picture of a man caught between his mother's wishes and his wife's wishes:

In your opinion,
a) When a man is caught between his mother and his wife, to whom should he give priority? _____

b) Why?

_____
_____
_____
_____
_____

6   With the help of question 3, fill the gaps below and memorize this important verse:

"That is why a man leaves his father and mother and is united to his wife, and they become _____ _____"   (Genesis 2:24)

7   God's design for marriage is one man united with one woman, for their whole life. One time some religious people sought a legal opinion (*fatwa*) from Jesus Christ. They asked, *"Is it lawful for a man to divorce his wife for any and every reason?"*

Jesus quoted the verse you have just memorized. Then he continued *"So they are no longer two, but one flesh. Therefore what God has joined together, let no one separate."* (Matthew 19:3-6)

According to Christ's teaching, which one of the following statements is correct?
  ___ a) Marriage is merely a contract which two people make or break as they wish
  ___ b) Marriage is a binding commitment, joining two people into one

8   Yes, in God's sight two separate people become 'one' in marriage. Husband and wife should share this unity not just with their bodies but also with their hearts and minds.

What is God's design for marriage? One man united with ___ woman, for their whole life.

Come Follow Me

9   Can one man be fully united in heart and mind with two wives at the same time? No, this is impossible! Which of the following usually result when a man takes more than one wife? *(tick one or more answers, according to your own observation)*

      ___ a) the man treats one wife as his favourite
      ___ b) the other wives are jealous of the favourite one
      ___ c) there is harmony in the home
      ___ d) there may be too many children and they get neglected

10   God's design for marriage is <u>one</u> man united with <u>one</u> woman, for their <u>whole life</u>. This is strong teaching! Many people will not agree with it. Have you met men like this one below?

> I say that my wife is my 'field'. I sow my seed in the field. If my field is fruitless, I may get rid of it and take another. Or I might obtain another field, if I can afford it. I am the landowner and I may take whatever fields I like.

What differences do you see between this man's attitude and God's design for marriage? Note your ideas here and be ready for the discussion:

_____
_____
_____

11   Marriage is a precious gift from God. But God does not command everyone to get married. Jesus himself never married, and he said that some people choose not to marry.

Also we don't live in an ideal world and many people do not have an ideal marriage. In your opinion,
a) Does God feel the pain of those who are in an unhappy marriage?   [Yes / No]
b) Does God feel the pain of those who lost their spouse through death or divorce? [Yes / No]
c) Does God feel the pain of those who are single but would love to be married?   [Yes / No]

> Review: Let's summarise what we have learned so far:
> - Men and women have equal value in God's sight;
> - God created wives as companions to their husbands, not as servants;
> - God's design for marriage is: one man united with one woman for their whole life.
>
> To have a happy married life, let's put these principles into practice!

Lesson Eleven

Husbands and Wives in 1 Peter

12   As we have seen, God sets a high standard for our married lives. But we often fail to reach to God's standard, because we are selfish. 1 Peter chapter 3 tells us how to strengthen our marriage by overcoming our selfish attitudes.

Read 1 Peter 3:1-7 . Tick the box when you have done so ☐ .

13   Men and women have equal value in God's sight. However, God gave different responsibilities to husbands and wives, so that in marriage they could fit together perfectly and meet each other's needs. What are these responsibilities, according to 1 Peter 3?

- Responsibility of Wives: "_____ yourselves to your own husbands" *(1 Peter 3:1)*
- Responsibility of Husbands: "Be _____ as you live with your wives" *(1 Peter 3:7)*

Responsibility of Wives

14   Wives are told to *"submit"*. This is not easy if your husband is unkind or selfish. But, wives, remember that we submit *"for the Lord's sake"* (1 Peter 2:13).

For whose sake will a believing wife submit to her husband? The _____'s sake.

15   Some cultures expect a wife to live as her husband's slave and never express her own opinion. But the Bible does not teach this. As we learned earlier, God created both men and women in his own image. Therefore in their marriage, both of their opinions are important.

However, 1 Peter 3:1-2 reminds the wife not to push for her own will in a selfish way. See what this woman says to her husband even though they have little money:

Do you expect me to wear these old clothes for my cousin's wedding? I need a new suit, and shoes to match!

What does this wife care more about? *(tick one)*
   ___ a) 'How can I please my husband?'
   ___ b) 'How can my husband please me?'

16   According to 1 Peter 3:3-4, she is making another mistake too. What is it? *(read the verses)* ___ a) She thinks true beauty comes from gold jewellery and fine clothes
   ___ b) She thinks true beauty comes from a gentle and quiet spirit

17   Instead of being selfish, what should wives do according to 1 Peter 3:1? '_____ yourselves to your own husbands'.

Come Follow Me

Responsibility of Husbands

18   If you are a man reading this lesson, maybe you are glad that your wife should submit to you. But 1 Peter chapter 3 puts an even more difficult responsibility on you than on your wife!

Read 1 Peter 3:7 again and fill the blanks: *"Husbands, in the same way be _____ as you live with your wives, and treat them with _____"*

19   Notice this verse says 'in the same way':

a) As we learned earlier, what should Christian wives care about more:
   ___ 1. 'How can I please my husband?' or
   ___ 2. 'How can my husband please me?'

b) Therefore, in the same way, what should Christian husbands care about more:
   ___ 1. 'How can I please my wife?' or
   ___ 2. 'How can my wife please me?'

20   Many men in this world assume that women exist merely to make them happy. Husbands, as Christ's follower your selfish attitude has to change! Compare these two men:

Jabbar: *I want to please my wife. I am grateful for all the work she does to take care of the house and children. I am willing to help her when she needs it.*

Tariq: *I want my wife to please me. She must cook delicious food, keep the house clean and take care of my children. She must not refuse me in bed either.*

a) Which man, Tariq or Jabbar, is considerate towards his wife? _____
b) Which man is selfish? _____
c) In your opinion, which of them is more manly? _____

21   The husband should be 'considerate'. He will never beat his wife. He will not neglect her or insult her. Instead he will sacrifice himself for her, to help her and build her up. This is manly. This is Christ-like.

Instead of being selfish, what should husbands do according to 1 Peter 3:7? 'Be _____ as you live with your wives'.

22   Husbands, as head of the household don't think that your wife always serves you and you should never serve her. Jesus Christ was head over his disciples, but still he served them and cared for them. He sacrificed himself for us. This is the model that we husbands should imitate, to sacrifice ourselves for our wives with Christ's love!

In your opinion, should husbands and wives ever share the housework? *(Write your opinion and be ready for discussion).*

_____
_____

If your Spouse is not yet in Christ...
23   It is very sad if only the wife is a believer, or only the husband. What advice does 1 Peter 3:1-2 give to Christian wives in this situation? *(tick one best answer below)*
        ___ a) keep nagging their husbands to become Christ's follower
        ___ b) refuse to share their bed until the husband turns to Christ
        ___ c) get divorced from their husbands
        ___ d) draw them towards Christ with the beauty of their lives

24   This advice in 1 Peter is also good for Christian husbands whose wives are not yet in Christ. Read this true account of an Afghan couple:

> Daud Jan became Christ's follower. His wife, Sharifa, opposed him at first. But she saw that his treatment of her changed. He even thanked her for the food she cooked! Now she too has entrusted herself to Jesus Christ.

If Christ's follower is patient and loving like Daud Jan, what do you think will be the effect on the non-Christian spouse? *(Write your opinion and be ready for discussion)*

_____

25   Often after one spouse turns to Christ, the other eventually follows. But this is not guaranteed. The non-believing partner may bring all kinds of pressure, insults or even divorce for the believer.

But according to Christ's teaching (see question 7) should his follower take the first step for divorce?   [Yes / No]

If your Spouse is already in Christ...
26   If your spouse is Christ's follower, then how fortunate you both are! 1 Peter 3:7 says that together you are 'heirs of the gracious gift of life' and partners in prayer. What are good ways to strengthen this joint partnership? *(tick one or more good answers, in your opinion)*
        ___ a) Pray and read the Bible with each other every day
        ___ b) Discuss together how to bring up the children
        ___ c) Share your joys and anxieties with each other
        ___ d) Spend more time chatting with your friends than with your spouse
        ___ e) Jointly train your children to be followers of Jesus

Come Follow Me

> Finally, think about your relationship with your own spouse (if you have one).
> - Is it a close friendship? Or is it more like a master/servant relationship?
> - What practical steps can you take to strengthen your partnership with your spouse?

LESSON 11 PRACTICAL TASK

Think of one thing you can do to make your spouse happy. Then <u>do</u> it this week.

Or if you are not married,

Ask a married person what they do to make their spouse happy.

LESSON 11 REVIEW

1 Write the memory verse:

"That is why a man _____
_____" (Genesis 2 : ___) *(see question 3)*

2 What is God's design for marriage? _____ man united with _____ woman for their _____ life.

3 Husbands and wives have equal value in God's sight, but different responsibilities.
a) What responsibility of the wife is mentioned in 1 Peter 3:1? '_____'
b) What responsibility of the husband is mentioned in 1 Peter 3:7? 'Be _____'

4 Being selfish, we usually think 'How can my spouse please me?' But as Christ's followers what should we care more about? 'How can _____ please my spouse?"

LESSON 11 ANSWERS

1. b)
2. a) True   b) False   c) False   d) True
3. a) mother   b) wife
4. a)
5. for discussion
6. memorize the verse
7. b)
8. one
9. in my experience, a) b) and d) are true. If your experience is different, bring it for discussion
10. for discussion
11. for discussion
12. read the passage then continue to the next question
13. submit, considerate
14. Lord
15. b)
16. a)
17. submit
18. considerate, respect
19. a) 1   b) 1
20. a) Jabbar   b) Tariq   c) for discussion
21. considerate
22. for discussion
23. d)
24. for discussion
25. No (unless the situation is desperate)
26. my suggestion is a), b), c), e)

Study tip: Write the memory verses on cards. Carry them with you and practise them through the day.

Lesson 12   <u>Solving our Disputes</u>

> We are God's chosen people. Therefore, we should love each other deeply. Our Lord Jesus said, *"Everyone will know that you are my disciples if you love one another"* (John 13:35).

> Yet even as Christ's followers, we sometimes have disputes. In this lesson we will learn how to solve these disputes. When we manage to do so, the bonds of love between us grow even stronger than before.

Disputes among Christ's Followers

1   In every earthly family, there are sometimes disputes between brothers or jealousy between sisters. This happens too in our spiritual family of Christ's church. In heaven our spiritual family will be perfect, but it is not yet perfect here on earth.

a) Has a brother or sister in Christ ever caused hurt to you?   [Yes / No]
b) Have you ever caused hurt to a brother or sister in Christ?   [Yes / No]

2   Even at the time of the apostle Peter, the believers sometimes had disputes. See what advice the apostle Peter gave to them. Read 1 Peter 3:8-12 and fill the gaps from verse 8: *"Finally, all of you, be like-minded, be sympathetic, _____ one another, be compassionate and _____ ."*

3   When they learned to solve their disputes, their love grew even stronger.

Mark the following statements 'True' or 'False':
    _____ a) God's chosen people on this earth are always perfect
    _____ b) Christ's followers sometimes have disputes
    _____ c) Christ's followers can solve their disputes and be reconciled

4   Some disputes of those early believers were similar to our disputes today. For instance:

- One group of believers complained that another group was receiving more aid money than them (Acts 6:1-6)
- One group criticized the apostle Peter for breaking their ethnic customs (Acts 11:1-18)Two groups disagreed about what religious customs Christ's followers must follow (Acts 15:1-32)

On each of those occasions the believers found a way to solve their dispute and restore peace with each other. They followed the advice of their leader Peter:

Now memorize the following verse.

> *"They must seek peace and pursue it"* (1 Peter 3:11)

5   In your experience, what things cause disputes among Christ's followers today? Tick one or more of the following, according to your own observation:

    ___ a) one believer causes offence to another
    ___ b) one person is jealous that another has more money
    ___ c) two people compete to lead the group of believers
    ___ d) Christ's followers disagree over doctrine
    ___ e) believers pass on gossip about each other
    ___ f) another cause, such as _____
                          (give an example from your own experience)

God longs for us to solve our disputes

6   Whenever God sees us divided by disputes, it grieves him very much. He longs for us to be reconciled to each other. The Lord Jesus taught that this is even more important than attending worship (Matthew 5:23-24).

What is our Saviour's attitude whenever there are disputes among his chosen people? *(tick two correct answers)*

    ___ a) It makes him very sad
    ___ b) It does not affect him at all
    ___ c) He longs for us to solve our disputes

> God longs for us to solve our disputes and be reconciled. But how practically can we do this? There are bad ways and good ways. Let's learn first about some bad ways.

Bad Ways to Solve Disputes

7   One bad way to solve disputes is to <u>fight</u>. Some people fight with fists, some with Kalashnikovs. Some fight in the law-courts and some in their homes. But what does this lead to, according to what we learned in lesson 10?
    ___ a) reconciliation   ___ b) revenge

8   Another bad way to solve disputes is to <u>turn our backs</u> on each other. People cut each other off and refuse to talk with each other. They even prevent their families from having any contact with each other.

Sometimes this state of isolation continues for years and years. What are the negative results, in your experience? _____
_____
_____

9   A third bad way to solve disputes is to <u>enforce surrender</u>. The stronger person forces the weaker person to give way. If a mediator is asked to help, he typically takes the side of the senior person without tackling the issue fairly. So the junior person has to surrender and say the words 'I apologize' even when he does not mean it.

On the surface this appears to solve the dispute, but:
a) Has justice really been done? [Yes / No]
b) Will the junior person still feel resentment in his heart? [Yes / No]
c) Does true reconciliation take place? [Yes / No]

10   Tackling disputes through 'enforced surrender' brings peace on the surface, but it is not true deep peace. A wife may surrender to her husband, but their hearts will remain divided. In the church, a younger leader may surrender to the elder one, but he may continue to spread discontent among the believers and later the group will split.

Can fighting, turning our backs or forcing a surrender bring true peace? _____

A better way to solve disputes

Now let us learn a better way to solve our disputes. This way involves three steps:
First step: Bring your emotions to God
Second step: Talk with the other person
Third step: Give and receive forgiveness

First Step: Bring your emotions to God
11   When we have a dispute with someone we feel strong emotions against that person. Hurt, anger and desire for revenge fill up our minds so completely that there is no room left for any other thoughts!

If we go to confront the other person while our thoughts are still full of anger, we will definitely use angry words. Then in turn the other person will defend himself with angry words too.

In such a state, will that person be able to consider calmly anything we say? [Yes / No]

12   Therefore, as the first step we need to bring our angry emotions to God. He listens while we pour out our emotions to him. He is our Healer, so we should show him our spiritual wounds just as a patient shows his bodily wounds to the doctor.

What is the first step towards solving our disputes? Bring your _____ to God.

13 As we keep talking with God about these negative emotions, he will gradually reduce the anger in our minds. That makes room for other thoughts to enter, like this:

"The other person was in the wrong, but maybe I was a little in the wrong too."

"And since Christ forgave me so much, shouldn't I forgive the other person too?"

Probably we are not yet completely free of the anger. But slowly our emotions have come under control sufficiently for us to be able to speak calmly with the other person. We also ask God to prepare that person to be willing to listen to us. We wait for the right opportunity to meet with them.

What is the first step towards solving our disputes? Bring your emotions to _____

Second Step: Talk with the other person

14 Here Ali and Karim are two followers of Christ. They have a dispute. Ali speaks first:

1 Brother Karim, when you didn't invite me to your daughter's wedding, I was deeply upset. Can you imagine how much dishonour this caused me?

2 Believe me, brother Ali, I fully intended to invite you. But in those days I was so busy it just slipped out of my mind. It was a serious mistake.

But I too felt hurt when afterwards you complained about me to our friends. Why didn't you talk with me instead?

Ali *Karim*

Come Follow Me

a) Are they discussing in a calm or angry way?   _____
b) Are they listening carefully to each other?   _____

15   Ali had previously completed the first step by bringing his emotions to God. So now in the second step he is able to talk about the problem without getting angry again. Calmly he explains how Karim hurt him. Karim listens carefully without interrupting. Then Karim explains how Ali hurt him, and Ali listens without interrupting.

     They both describe their feelings honestly, but in a loving way. They are *"speaking the truth in love"*, as Ephesians 4:15 says. They are making good progress towards solving their dispute.

What is the second step in solving our disputes?   [Talk / fight] with the other person
(circle the correct answer)

16   Also, notice that Ali does not attack or insult Karim's <u>person</u>. Instead he just focuses on Karim's specific <u>action</u>. This is important to remember whenever we have a dispute with someone. Therefore:

a) Which sentence below, 1. or 2., is better for a wife to say to her husband? _____
    1. 'The meat you bought yesterday was too expensive, could you try a different
       butcher next time?'
    2. 'You are so wasteful, you always waste our money!'
b) Why do you think this? _____

17   But earlier Ali had made a mistake. He had complained about Karim to his friends instead of going to talk directly with Karim in private. Our Lord Jesus gave us this guidance:

> "If your brother or sister sins, go and point out their fault, just between the two of you. If they listen to you, you have won them over."   (Matthew 18:15)

Why is it so important to speak in private? *(write your own opinion and be ready for discussion)*
_____
_____

18   Let's check if Ali and Karim are using any of the bad ways to solve their dispute that we learned earlier in this lesson:

a) Are Ali and Karim <u>fighting</u> with each other?   [Yes / No]
b) Are they <u>turning their backs</u> on each other?   [Yes / No]
c) Is one of them <u>forcing</u> the other to <u>surrender</u>?   [Yes / No]

19   They are tackling their dispute in a good way! Write here the two steps they have taken so far:
    First Step: Bring your _____ to God
    Second Step: _____ with the other person

20   Now Ali and Karim come to the third step.

Third Step: Give and Receive Forgiveness

This time Karim speaks first:

1 Brother Ali, I am sincerely sorry I failed to invite you to the wedding. I recognise this was a big insult to you. Please forgive me.

2 Yes, I forgive you! And please forgive me too. I hurt your reputation by complaining to other people. I am sorry, brother Karim.

Ali   *Karim*

In this conversation,

a) Which of them apologizes? *(tick one only)*
　　___ 1. Ali　　___ 2. Karim　　___ 3. Both of them　　___ 4. Neither of them

b) What position do they each take? *(tick one only)*
　　___ 1. 'Nothing was my fault'
　　___ 2. 'Everything was my fault'
　　___ 3. 'I apologize for the part that was my fault'

21   Neither Ali nor Karim just surrenders to the other, saying 'everything was my fault'. Instead they recognize that 'one hand does not make a clap' and so:
- Ali apologizes specifically for what was his fault
- Karim apologizes specifically for what was his fault

It is hard to ask someone to forgive us, isn't it? This is not a weak thing to do. Rather, it takes manly strength to do such a hard thing.

What is the third step in solving our disputes? _____ and _____ forgiveness.

22   We should be

> "forgiving each other, just as in Christ God forgave you"   (Ephesians 4:32).

God has forgiven and buried our past sins. In the same way when we forgive someone for a particular sin, we should bury it. After burying it, we should never dig it up again!

But what if that person repeats the same offence in future? Should we forgive them again? The apostle Peter asked this same question. Read Jesus' reply in Matthew 18:21-22. *(You can find Matthew's gospel in your Bible in the 'List of Contents')*

How many times did Jesus tell Peter to forgive? _____

23   Watch now as Karim and Ali give and receive forgiveness. What joy these two brothers in Christ feel when they are reconciled!

Stop and think:
> ➤ *Are you in a dispute with a brother or sister in Christ? Would you like the joy of being reconciled to them? Ask God to prepare the way for this to happen.*

Sometimes, even when we ourselves try to give and receive forgiveness in a dispute, the other person might not be willing. This makes reconciliation impossible until their attitude changes. But at least let us try our best from our side. God's Word says, *"If it is possible, so far as it depends on you, live at peace with everyone"* (Rom 12:18).

LESSON 12 PRACTICAL TASK

In question 23, you thought about someone with whom you need reconciliation. Each day this week, talk with God about this person. Use this prayer:

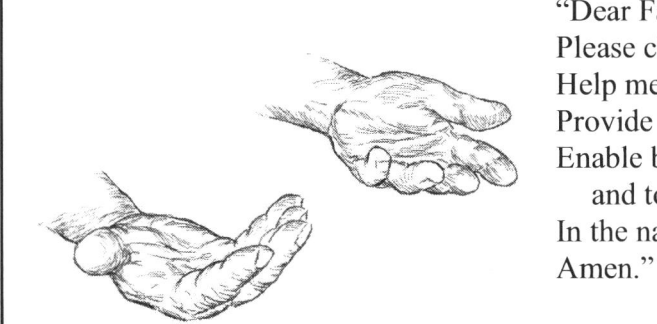

"Dear Father God,
Please change my emotions about [name].
Help me understand his/her point of view.
Provide a suitable opportunity to talk with him/her.
Enable both of us to listen to each other
  and to forgive each other.
In the name of the Lord Jesus who forgave me,
Amen."

LESSON 12 REVIEW

1 These pictures show three ways people often try to solve disputes. Write by each one 'good' or 'bad':

_____ a) fight   _____ b) turn our backs   _____ c) enforce surrender

2 Write three good steps to solve our disputes:
First Step: Bring your _____ to God
Second Step: _____ with the other person
Third Step: _____ and _____ _____

3 Write the memory verse, with its reference:

"They must seek _____" (1 Peter ___:___)

LESSON 12 ANSWERS

1. a), b) personal answers. Probably all of us have been hurt by other followers of Christ, but probably we have all hurt them too.
2. love, humble
3. a) False   b) True   c) True
4. memorize the verse
5. personal answers, for discussion time
6. a), c)
7. b)
8. for discussion time
9. a) No b) Yes c) No
10. No
11. No
12. emotions
13. God
14. a) Yes b) Yes
15. talk
16. a) 1. b) because sentence 1. is about her husband's specific action, while sentence 2. is a general attack on him personally
17. for discussion time
18. a) No b) No c) No
19. emotions, talk
20. a) 3. b) 3.
21. give, receive
22. seventy-seven, i.e. so many you lose count!
23. stop and pray

Study tip: It is very important to answer the questions which ask your personal opinion. Please don't miss them out!

Lesson 13   <u>Giving Witness</u>

Mehdi Dibaj was a pastor in Iran. The government put him in prison for nine long years. Finally, in December 1993, they brought him to trial on the charge of apostasy.

> *If you were an old man, after nine years in prison, wouldn't you long to be free? This would be so easy – just by disowning Christ and returning to your old religion.*

Medhi Dibaj gave courageous testimony in front of the whole court.   Here are some extracts from his actual speech:

"I have been charged with 'apostasy' [rejecting my faith]...
I would rather have the whole world against me, but know the Almighty God is with me; be called an apostate, but know I have the approval of the God of glory.

They tell me, 'Return!' [to my former religion]. But from the arms of my God, who can I return to?... It is now 45 years that I am walking with the God of miracles, and his kindness upon me is like a shadow...The love of Jesus has filled all my being and I feel the warmth of his love in every part of my body.

Life for me is an opportunity to serve Christ, and death is a better opportunity to be with him. Therefore I am not only satisfied to be in prison for the honour of his Holy Name, but am ready to give my life for the sake of Jesus my Lord and enter his kingdom sooner.

With respect,

Your Christian prisoner,   Mehdi Dibaj"

Do you want to know what the outcome of Mehdi Dibaj's trial was? You will have to wait until the group meeting!. But now let's learn how we can give witness for Christ.

Come Follow Me

Giving Witness for Christ

1	1 Peter 3:14-15 tells us three important guidelines for our witness. Read the verses and fill the blanks:

a) "Do not be _____. But in your hearts set apart Christ as Lord"
b) "Always be _____ to give an answer to everyone who asks you"
c) "But do this with _____ and respect."

2	Come, let's learn about each of these guidelines.

A) 'Do not be Frightened'
We are naturally frightened about how our friends and relatives will react when they discover we are Christ's followers. Have you personally felt that fear? _____

3	God says:

"Do not be frightened"　　　　　　(1 Peter 3:14)

Fear holds us back from making spiritual progress. But when we break through the barrier of fear, it sets us free:

In a country in North Africa, some young people had become Christ's followers but they kept this a secret. They feared that their parents would find out. But later the police heard about these young people and threatened them, "If you persist in your new religion, we will tell your parents".

The young believers remained faithful to Jesus, and the police told their parents. They suffered some persecution after that. But they grew much stronger in trusting their Lord, because they had survived the very thing that they had feared the most!

What guideline of giving witness did these young believers learn through experience?
'Do not be _____'

4	1 Peter 3:14-15 continues, *"Do not be frightened. But in your hearts revere Christ as Lord"*. To revere Christ as Lord means honouring him as our Ruler, not anyone else.

If we revere Christ as Lord, should we deny we are his followers? [Yes / No]

5	In principle, we should openly give witness for Christ. But sometimes our circumstances make this very difficult. Perhaps you feel the time is not yet right to tell your loved ones about your faith in Jesus Christ.
　　This may be wise for a period of time. But it should only be a temporary stage, on the path towards giving open witness. We should not remain secret forever! Those who do so, almost always grow weaker spiritually.

Therefore, which of the prayers below is better, A or B? _____

"O Lord, may my family members never find out that I am your follower."

"O Lord, please prepare my family members to hear about Christ when the time is right. And, when that time comes, help me not to be frightened"

6   In John's gospel we read about a man called 'Joseph of Arimathea'. He was Jesus' follower. At first he remained a secret believer because of his circumstances. But later, at the time of testing, he publicly proved loyal to Christ (John 19:38).
       By contrast, the apostle Peter boasted of his loyalty to Jesus. But at his time of testing, out of fear he publicly denied being Christ's follower. Afterwards he deeply regretted this and 'wept bitterly' (Luke 22:62).

So, when we face our time of testing, should we be like Joseph or Peter? _____

7   Some of us are still secret believers, but in due time we too will face the test. At that time, we will take strength from this promise of our Lord Jesus:

"On account of me you will stand before governors and kings as witnesses to them... Whenever you are arrested and brought to trial, do not worry beforehand about what to say. Just say whatever is given you at the time, for it is not you speaking, but the Holy Spirit"
(Mark 13:9,11)

This reminds us of the first guideline for giving witness, from 1 Peter 3:14-15. What is it? "Do not be _____"

If you are still a secret follower of Christ, talk about it with your advisor. Above all talk with God, for by his Spirit he will guide you what to do.

Come Follow Me

B) 'Be Prepared to Give an Answer'

8   The apostle Peter wrote *"be prepared to give an answer"*. People might ask us questions like these:

A — Why do you call Jesus the Son of God? That is blasphemy! (or *shirk*)

B — Why did you betray the faith of your ancestors and follow a western religion?

C — The Bible has been changed, so why do you believe it?

Pick <u>one</u> of these questions, whichever one you like; think about how you would answer it.

Which person's question have you chosen? _____ *(write the letter)*
What answer would you give? _____

_____
_____
_____

(Just note down a few ideas, they need not be perfect. We will discuss this more together).

9   Some people are spiritually closed. They ask questions merely to attack our beliefs and to trip us up. We should be careful in speaking with those people and not say too much.

But other people are more open. They genuinely want us to '*give the reason for the hope that you have*', like the lady in this picture:

Why are you happier than before?

What answer would you give her?

_____
_____

90

10   We should 'be prepared to give an answer' to those who have genuine questions. We should be ready to explain the good news of Christ in a simple way. Some key points of our message come in 1 Peter 3:18:

> "For Christ also suffered once for sins, the righteous for the unrighteous, to bring you to God"   (1 Peter 3:18)

Repeat this verse until it is firm in your memory.

11   Our non-Christian friends think that Jesus Christ came to this earth only to give 'right guidance'. But we long for them to know his real purpose! What was it? "... to bring you to _____" *(see the verse above)*

12   Write the verse again from memory:

"For Christ _____ ,
_____" (1 Peter ___ : ___)

13   Suppose your friend or family member asks you this question:

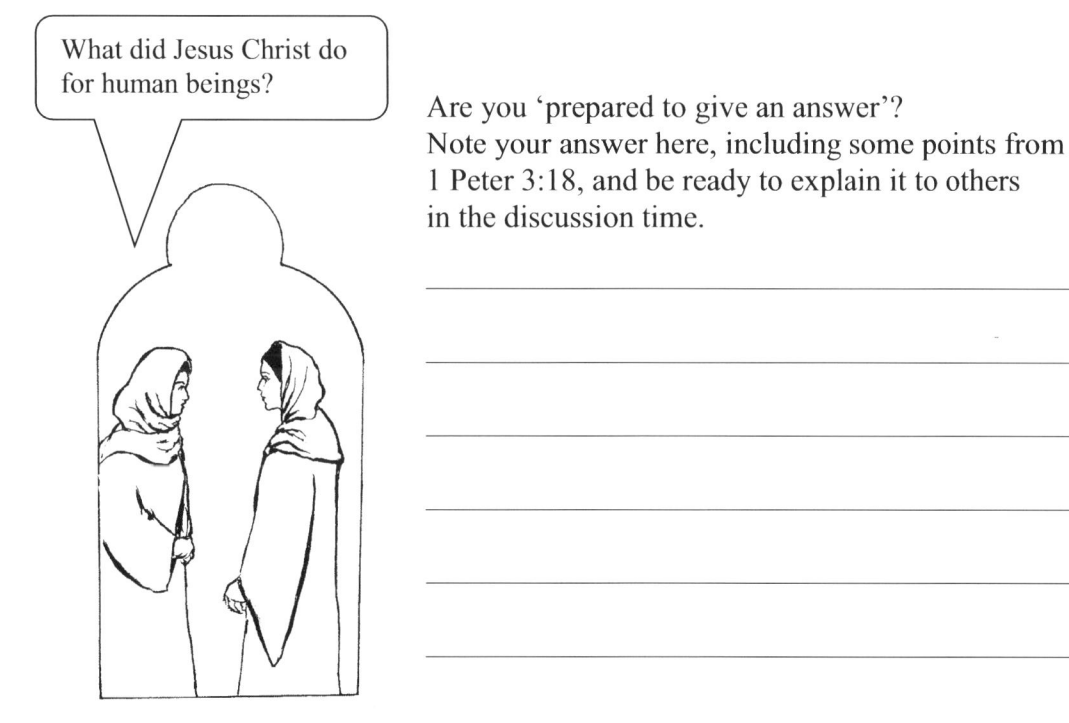

What did Jesus Christ do for human beings?

Are you 'prepared to give an answer'?
Note your answer here, including some points from
1 Peter 3:18, and be ready to explain it to others
in the discussion time.

_____
_____
_____
_____
_____

C) 'With Gentleness and Respect'

14   Let's read 1 Peter 3:14-15 once more:

> "Do not be frightened. But in your hearts revere Christ as Lord. Always be prepared to give an answer to everyone who asks you to give the reason for the hope that you have. But do this with gentleness and respect"   (1 Peter 3:14-15)

According to this verse, which of the following is the best way to speak about Christ to our relatives and friends? *(tick one)*

____ a) Speak openly about Jesus but in a disrespectful way
____ b) Be ready to speak about Jesus, with gentleness and respect
____ c) Don't speak at all about Jesus even when we are asked

Come Follow Me

15   As 'God's chosen people', we should show gentleness and respect. If we argue and quarrel with non-Christians, we will only build up bigger barriers.

Therefore, how should we give witness? With gentleness and _____.

16   Read this true account:

> Saleem was a young man when he received Christ. His non-Christian brothers were very angry with him. They tried to persuade him to return to his old religion but he carefully explained his reasons for following Christ. Saleem's brothers set fire to his house, but he managed to escape. Then they gave him poison and he nearly died.
>
> After this he moved to another city, but he kept in contact with his brothers and sisters. He sent greetings at Eid and helped financially when they were sick. Gradually, seeing his love their attitude began to change. Today they are still not followers of Jesus, but they trust and respect Saleem. But this change took 20 years!

Which one answer below describes how Saleem gave witness to his loved ones?
   ___ a) Saleem was 'prepared to give an answer' but not 'with gentleness and respect'
   ___ b) Saleem showed 'gentleness and respect' but was not 'prepared to give an answer'
   ___ c) Saleem showed 'gentleness and respect' and also was 'prepared to give an answer'

17   Yes, Saleem followed the guidelines of 1 Peter 3:15. He was bold in his witness but also gentle and respectful. This is hard to do, especially for those who live at home under their parents. We wonder how far should we compromise and go along with their wishes.

For instance, what would you do in the following circumstances?

? Suppose your father commands you to throw away your Bible...

? Or your mother pleads, with tears, that you stop meeting with Christians...

? Or your parents want you to marry your non-Christian cousin?

Think about what you would do in these difficult situations, and be ready for discussion.

18   If at all possible, it is best not to run away from our families. We should try to stay, and respect our parents, and earn money to contribute to the household. By our actions as well as our words, what will we show? *(tick two answers)*

   ___ a) gentleness   ___ b) respect   ___ c) pride   ___ d) rebellion

The Bread of Life

19   In telling other people about the Lord Jesus Christ, we don't have to be experts. As someone said, it's just like *"one beggar telling another beggar where to find bread"*. Any beggar knows how to do that!

Jesus Christ is the Bread of Life. He has satisfied our spiritual hunger. But how will our loved ones also have this opportunity? *(tick one)*

   ___ a) if we remain secret believers
   ___ b) if we give witness for Christ only through our deeds not through our words
   ___ c) if we give witness for Christ in our words as well as our deeds

20   Read this true account:

> An Afghan man was Christ's follower for many years but did not tell his wife. Later she received Christ herself through the witness of her friend. Afterwards she was astonished to find he too was a believer. "Why didn't you tell me earlier?" she exclaimed.

If we have the 'bread of life', should we deny it to our loved ones?   [Yes/No]

> How can we refuse the 'bread of life' to hungry people? Our Lord Jesus Christ offers to satisfy their hunger eternally. Let's ask God to guide us to those who have genuine spiritual hunger and let's have the courage to tell them.

LESSON 13 PRACTICAL TASK

Think of one person you want to tell about the good news of Jesus Christ. Ask God to make that person ready to listen. Then look out for an opportunity to show or tell him/her just a little of what Christ has done for you.

LESSON 13 REVIEW

1   1 Peter 3:14 15 gives three guidelines on how to witness for Christ. What are they?
    a) "Do not be _____"
    b) "Always be _____ to give an answer"
    c) "But do this with _____ and _____."

2   Look at these two believers:

   ❖ *Nadia*'s sister asks her why she has accepted Jesus. Nadia replies *"I don't really know, I can't tell you."*
   ❖ *Anwar* says to his father, *"If you don't become a follower of Jesus you will go to hell"*.

   a) Which guideline for witness has Nadia forgotten?
   'Be _____ to give an _____'
   b) Which guideline for witness has Anwar forgotten?
   'With _____ and _____'

3   Write the memory verse:
   "For Christ _____,
   _____, _____" (1 Peter ___:___)

Come Follow Me

LESSON 13 ANSWERS

1. read the verses to find the answer
2. personal answer
3. frightened
4. No
5. B
6. Joseph
7. frightened
8. be ready for discussion
9. personal answer
10. memorize the verse
11. God
12. write the verse from memory
13. be ready for discussion
14. b)
15. respect
16. c)
17. for discussion
18. a) and b) are correct
19. c)
20. No

Study tip: Head knowledge is not enough. Ask God to change your heart too.

Lesson 14   Baptism

This young man Hamid is puzzled. Last year he entrusted his life to Jesus Christ. He is growing stronger in his new faith. Recently another believer told him, "Soon you should be baptized". This started many questions in Hamid's mind:

- What is baptism?
- Is baptism very important?
- Why should I get baptized?
- What does baptism show?
- When should I get baptized?

Hamid

Let's try to answer each of Hamid's questions in today's lesson.

'What is Baptism?'
1   'Baptism' literally means getting dipped or plunged in water. In the New Testament we read how John the Baptist (*Yahya*) baptized people in the river Jordan, including even Jesus himself. These days Christ's followers may be baptized in a river or tank, going right down under the water for a few moments. An alternative way is to pour or sprinkle water on them.

We go through this important ceremony just once, not repeatedly through our lives. What is the name of this ceremony? _____

'Why should I get Baptized?'
2   We get baptized because the Lord Jesus commanded it. He said

| "Go and make disciples of all nations, baptizing them in the name of the Father and of the Son and of the Holy Spirit".   (Matthew 28:19) |

This is an important verse. Please memorize it now.

3   In obedience to Christ's command, the apostle Peter told a huge crowd in Jerusalem *"Repent and be baptized"* (Acts 2:38). That day three thousand people accepted his message and took the step of baptism!

What is the best reason for me to get baptized? *(tick one only)*
    ___ a) because I want to do it
    ___ b) because my Christian friends want me to do it
    ___ c) because the Lord Jesus commands me to do it

Come Follow Me

'What does Baptism show?'

> Baptism is very special and significant. According to the New Testament, baptism shows that:
> A. I am a new person in Christ
> B. My sins are washed away
> C. I have joined Christ's community
> Let's learn now about these wonderful truths.

A) I am a New Person in Christ

4   Some people are afraid to go under the water in baptism. Don't worry, during baptism people go under the water only for a few seconds and it is not dangerous. But it is a meaningful symbol of what happens to us when we turn to Christ. It is like our old sinful nature being drowned in the water so that we can rise up again to a new life in Jesus!

Draw lines to match the actions below with their related meaning:

Action	Meaning
a) Going down into the water	1. I rise again as a new person in Christ
b) Coming up out of the water	2. My old nature is put to death

5   So, baptism is a sign that my old life is finished and now I am a new person in Christ. God's Word says,

> "We were therefore buried with him through baptism into death in order that, just as Christ was raised from the dead through the glory of the Father, we too may live a new life"
> (Romans 6:4)

What is the first truth that baptism shows? *(circle the correct answer)*
    [I am a new person in Christ / I am still in my old, sinful nature]

6   Often at a baptism people go down into the water wearing their old clothes symbolizing their old sinful life. Then they come up out of the water and put on fresh clean clothes showing their new life in Christ.

> *If you have already been baptized, what were your emotions when you came out of the water? Be ready to talk about this in the discussion time.*

7   Firaz from Africa came to Christ from the same previous religion as you. Here he describes, in his own words, what he felt after his baptism:

> "I felt I have died to my old sinful way, I have given myself to God and am now a new person. I am not the Firaz my friends knew, not the one whom Satan knew, but a new Firaz - forgiven, born again, controlled by the Spirit. The old Firaz is dead, the new one is alive in Christ. I came out of the water feeling I am a new person!"

In the box above, how many times did Firaz use the phrase 'new'? ____ Underline them.

8   What is the first truth that baptism shows? I am a _____ person in Christ

B) My Sins are Washed Away

9   Acts 22:16 tells us about a second truth about baptism: *"be baptized and wash your sins away"*.

According to this verse, what truth does baptism show?
(tick one)
   ___ a) I am a new person in Christ
   ___ b) My sins are washed away

10   As we know from our own experience, ablutions (*wudu*) or even a full bath (*ghusal*) is not enough to wash away our sins. Water can only wash the outside of our bodies, it cannot cleanse our hearts and consciences.

Nevertheless, baptism is a powerful <u>outward sign</u> of the <u>inner cleansing</u> which Christ does in our hearts. He died on the cross to make this possible. Read 1 John 1:7 *(note that 1 John is a different book of the Bible from John. Check in your List of Contents).*

According to 1 John 1:7, what purifies us from all sin? _____

11   The apostle Peter, who baptized many people during his life, also wrote about baptism in 1 Peter 3:18-22. This passage is not easy to interpret. But the main points are:
- Our salvation is through Jesus' sufferings (verse 18) and resurrection (verse 21)
- Water is a mark of this salvation for us (verse 21) as it was for Noah (verse 20)

Which ceremony reminds me that my sins are washed away?
   ___ a) my baptism   ___ b) my wedding   ___ c) my funeral

C)   I have joined Christ's Community

12   By getting baptized we publicly join Christ's worldwide community of believers (Christ's *ummah*). We are men and women from many different races, but all united *"for we were all baptized by one Spirit so as to form one body."* (1 Corinthians 12:13).

What is the third truth which baptism shows?
I have joined Christ's _____

13   Baptism is not something private just for you, but it involves the whole community of believers. They will witness your baptism ceremony, and at the end of it they may use words like this to welcome you:

> "We welcome you into the Lord's family. We are members together of the body of Christ; we are children together of the same heavenly Father; we are inheritors together of the kingdom of God. We welcome you."

> ➢ *How fortunate we are to be welcomed by 'God's chosen people'! Stop now to thank God for your brothers and sisters in Christ.*

Come Follow Me

14   What three truths does baptism show? *(fill the blank)*
   a) I am a _____ person in Christ
   b) My _____ are washed away
   c) I have _____ Christ's community

Hamid is excited to learn these truths. Next he asks:

'Is Baptism very important?'
15   In one way it is not essential for salvation, for we are saved through trusting Christ not through water. But still, baptism is Christ's command! And as we have seen, it is a very important sign of belonging to him and to his church. So you should get baptized, when the time is right.

a) In many cultures, if you see a wedding ring on someone's finger what does it show?
_____

b) A ring is not totally essential for being married; but it is still an important sign that a person is committed to whom? _____

c) Likewise, our baptism is an important mark of commitment that we belong to whom?
_____

16   Through baptism we show we are proud to belong to our master Jesus Christ. And we are glad to tell this to our brothers and sisters in Christ. You will probably be asked to 'give your testimony' at your baptism. This means briefly telling everybody how Jesus Christ has changed your life.

Let's try this now. Imagine you are giving your testimony at your baptism. When the leader asks "What changes has Jesus Christ made in your life?", what will you say?
Write what you will say and be ready for discussion. If you wish, check what you wrote for Lesson 2 question 15. But write it here in more detail.
_____
_____
_____
_____

17   Salma's circumstances don't allow her to get baptized yet. Which would be better advice to give her, a) or b)?

___ a) 'Don't bother about it, baptism is unimportant'

___ b) 'Baptism is very important, so keep asking God to make it possible for your baptism to happen at the right time'

> In this lesson, we have tried to answer Hamid's different questions about baptism. Now we come to his last question.

Lesson Fourteen

'When should I get Baptized?'

18	Some Christians advise you to take baptism as soon as you receive Christ. Others say it is better to wait for some time until your faith is stronger. Listen to their advice, but listen to God's Spirit also. God himself will guide you in this important step. When the time is right, you will feel it in your heart.

Don't let humans rush you into getting baptized if you are not ready. But don't hang back either, if God is telling you now is the right time.

Which of the actions below are good? *(tick two answers)*
    ___ a) listen to the advice of wise believers who care for you
    ___ b) avoid getting baptized because you fear the consequences
    ___ c) think it is unimportant to get baptized
    ___ d) get baptized when you feel God telling you

19	Wise believers care for you and will give good advice about baptism. But some believers are unwise in making baptism arrangements, and some church leaders take advantage of baptisms to promote their own name. So find someone you trust to make arrangements for your baptism.

If you know who can give you good advice about your own baptism, tick this box ☐. If you don't know a suitable person, ask your advisor.

20	We thought earlier about what baptism means for us believers. But what does it mean for our non-Christian relatives? For them it is a sign that we publicly cut ourselves off from them, causing them hurt and shame.

How then should we take baptism?
    ___ a) Fearfully, worried for our own safety
    ___ b) Carefully, out of love for our families

21	Because of our non-Christian relatives, it is wise to be careful and take precautions. What precautions can you think of, to make sure that news of our baptism would not cause too much embarrassment to our relatives? *(Note your ideas and be ready for discussion)*

_____
_____

22	What advice would you give to a believer whose wife or husband is not yet Christ's follower? Should the believer get baptized now, or wait hoping to do it later when their spouse turns to Christ? *(Note your ideas and be ready for discussion time.)*

_____
_____

> Although Hamid's baptism should be carried out with due precaution, it will be a time of great rejoicing! Even the angels will celebrate with him!

Come Follow Me

LESSON 14 PRACTICAL TASK

If you have not yet been baptized, go to talk about it with the person you named in question 19. Get their advice about when and how you should be baptized. Ask the Lord for his advice too.

LESSON 14 REVIEW

1 Write the memory verse: "Go and make disciples, _____
_____ (Matthew ___ : ___)

2 We learned that my baptism is a sign of three things. What are they?
   a) 'I am a new _____'
   b) 'My _____ are _____ away'
   c) 'I have joined Christ's _____'

3 How important is it to get baptized?

___ very important ___ not important

100

LESSON 14 ANSWERS

1. baptism
2. memorize the verse
3. c)
4. a) 2   b) 1
5. I am a new person, in Christ
6. your personal response
7. 4
8. new
9. b)
10. the blood of Jesus
11. a)
12. community
13. stop and thank God
14. a) new   b) sins   c) joined
15. a) that you are already married
    b) your husband or wife
    c) Christ
16. be ready to give your testimony in the group
17. b) is better
18. a) and d) are good
19. tick the box if you know a wise person to advise you
20. b)
21. for discussion
22. for discussion

Lesson 15   <u>The Straight Path</u>

Have you ever watched a drunk man trying to walk in a straight line? He can't do it, can he? Even if you tell him clearly which direction to walk, he is completely incapable to do so. He is addicted to alcohol which prevents him following a straight path.

It is the same, spiritually, for all human beings. God Almighty has sent very many prophets to tell us the Straight Path. Everyone knows what the Straight Path is. We have prayed so many times, "Guide us on the Straight Path". Yet in practice we have not walked straight. Why not? And what can we do about it? We will find out about this in today's lesson.

The Purpose of God's law

1   Long ago God's people were in slavery in Egypt, under the cruel Pharoah. God rescued them, and afterwards he gave them his law to guide them on the straight path.

Which event happened first?
   ___ a) God rescued his people
   ___ b) God gave them his law to guide them

2   Did God save his people because they obeyed his law? No, he saved them when they were helpless to save themselves. He saved them because of his great mercy and love.

Afterwards God gave his law to the people through the prophet Moses. God's law was good. It was a complete way of life to guide the people. But still there was a problem. This law did not by itself give people the strength to obey it. Again and again God sent prophets to remind his people, but still they did not obey.

Why did God's people not follow the straight path? *(tick one)*
   ___ a) because they did not know what was the straight path
   ___ b) because the law itself was bad
   ___ c) because they were addicted to sin

Why do People not follow the Straight Path?

3   God's law is good. But sadly, even when people know what the straight path is, they do not want to walk in it. This is because the intention (*ne-ah*) of their heart is crooked. And even if they <u>want</u> to walk straight and do good, they are not <u>able</u> to, because they are addicted to sin. Sin is like a drug. It prevents people from following God's straight path, like the intoxicated man at the start of this lesson.

In your opinion, what can rescue people from their addiction to sin? *(tick one)*
   ___ a) their own hard work
   ___ b) extra laws
   ___ c) extra prayers
   ___ d) God himself

4   Some people called Pharisees tried very hard to obey the law of Moses in every small detail. But even this effort to be religious gave rise to sinful attitudes, such as:
- Pride, because they thought they were better than non-religious people;
- Hypocrisy, because they obeyed the law outwardly but not in their hearts;
- Wrong priorities, because they observed the small details of the law but neglected its bigger purpose.

Religious people in every country are in danger of having these same attitudes. Therefore, can even religious people be addicted to sin? [Yes / No]

Clean and Unclean

5   The Pharisees were extremely careful to eat only *halal* (clean) food. But this did not make them clean inside. The Lord Jesus taught:

> "Nothing outside a man can make him 'unclean' by going into him. Rather, it is what comes out of a man that makes him 'unclean'... For from within, out of men's hearts, come evil thoughts, sexual immorality, theft, murder, adultery, greed, malice, deceit, lewdness, envy, slander, arrogance and folly. All these evils come from inside and make a man 'unclean'."
> (Mark 7:15-23)

In the passage above, underline all the different sins mentioned by Jesus, which come from inside and make people unclean.

6   People cannot follow God's good law because they are addicted to evil. Their hearts are unclean. God's Word says *"The heart is deceitful above all things and beyond cure."* (Jeremiah 17:9)

Explain Jeremiah 17:9 in your own words: _____

God's Cure for the unclean Heart

7   The human heart is 'beyond cure', as Jeremiah 17:9 says. So God planned a better solution. Long ago he promised a kind of 'heart transplant'. Read his promise here:

> "I will give you a new heart and put a new spirit in you; I will remove from you your heart of stone and give you a heart of flesh. And I will put my Spirit in you and move you to follow my decrees and be careful to keep my laws." (Ezekiel 36:26-27)

> ➤ *This promise is for each of us! Read aloud the verse again, but this time wherever it says 'you' add your own name afterwards, e.g. 'you, Ibrahim' or 'you, Ruhama'.*

8   Not only did God promise us these things, he has actually fulfilled his promise. He sent our saviour Jesus Christ to put 'a new heart and a new spirit' in us.

So when a person puts their faith in Jesus, what do they receive? A new heart and a new _____.

9   This 'new spirit' is the Holy Spirit, whom God puts into our lives when we become Christ's followers. The Holy Spirit makes our hearts new. Moreover, he makes us <u>willing</u> and <u>able</u> to walk in God's straight path. So, God fulfils his promise that *"I will put my Spirit in you and move you to follow my decrees and be careful to keep my laws"*.

According to God's Word,
a) Before receiving the Holy Spirit, were we able to follow God's straight path?
[Yes / No]

Come Follow Me

b) Now that we have received the Holy Spirit, are we <u>able</u> to follow God's straight path?
[Yes / No]
c) Does the Holy Spirit make us <u>willing</u> to follow God's straight path?   [Yes / No]

10   Who makes us both willing and able to follow God's straight path? The Holy _____

Living for God

11   Read 1 Peter 4:1-6 and fill the blanks from verse 2: "they do not live the rest of their earthly lives for _____, but rather for _____"

12   In the past we were slaves to sin. But Christ has set us free from our addiction to evil! For whom must we now live, according to 1 Peter 4:2?
    ___ a) for evil human desires   ___ b) for God

13   Look at the list of sins in 1 Peter 4:3 – *"debauchery, lust, drunkenness, orgies, carousing and detestable idolatry"*. Maybe you think 'These are big sins, but I am not guilty of those. I only do small sins and God overlooks them'.

But no sin is small in God's sight. Take 'lust' for example. Our master Jesus Christ said:

> "You have heard that it was said, 'You shall not commit adultery.' But I tell you that anyone who looks at a woman lustfully has already committed adultery with her in his heart."
> (Matthew 5:27-28)

According to Christ's holy standard,
a) If a man thinks about sleeping with a beautiful girl, but does not actually do so, is this sin?   [Yes / No]
b) If I have the intention (*ne-ah*) for a sin but do not act on it, is this still sin?   [Yes / No]

14   Christ's law sets an extremely high standard. Remember, Jesus looks right inside into our heart like an x-ray looks inside a person. If we say our ritual prayers correctly but still tell lies, are we obeying Christ's law?   [Yes / No]

15   What kinds of sin does Christ's law forbid? *(tick any correct answers)*
    ___ a) major sins
    ___ b) minor sins
    ___ c) sinful actions (such as beating my wife)
    ___ d) sinful words (such as telling lies)
    ___ e) sinful thoughts (such as planning revenge)

16   In your opinion, which of the following actions are important in Christ's law?
        (by each one write 'Yes', 'No' or 'Not sure').
    _____ a) having a beard
    _____ b) being holy in all we do
    _____ c) loving one another deeply
    _____ d) performing the correct actions for ritual prayer
    _____ e) ridding ourselves of deceit and envy
    _____ f) wearing clothes which show we are religious
    _____ g) being compassionate and humble

Lesson Fifteen

True Freedom

17   Some so-called 'Christians' say,

"Christ has set me free, so I can do whatever I like! The more I sin, the more he will forgive me!"

This attitude is totally wrong! What answer would you give to this man, from 1 Peter 4:2-3? Note your ideas here, and be ready for discussion: _____
_____
_____

18   Yes, Christ set us free from our addiction and slavery to sin. But what kind of freedom does this give us? *(tick one)*
   ___ a) freedom to live for ourselves
   ___ b) freedom to live for God

19   Look at this man.

See how free I am! I am free to do whatever I like!

(hot temper, cheating in business, seeking revenge, pride)

Is he truly free or not? Why? *(note your ideas and be ready for discussion)*
_____
_____

105

Come Follow Me

20   If we live for ourselves, this is not true freedom. It is slavery to sin. Jesus Christ said *"everyone who sins is a slave to sin"* (John 8:34). The only place to break our chains is at the cross of Christ.

Christ paid a great ransom to buy us back from slavery. He paid with his own blood.

Therefore, to whom do we now belong? *(tick one)*

___ a) to ourselves   ___ b) to sin   ___ c) to Christ

21   Memorize this verse:

| "You are not your own, you were bought at a price. Therefore honour God with your bodies"   (1 Corinthians 6:19-20) |

22   We belong to Christ our master, who bought us. As his slaves we find true freedom – freedom from sin! This sounds strange but it is true.

Only one of the following people is able to walk on the straight path. Which one?)

___ a) the person who lives to please himself
___ b) the person who tries hard by his own efforts to obey God's law
___ c) the person who lives as a slave to Christ and is filled with the Holy Spirit

Never consider it a burden to obey Christ's law and to follow the straight path. It is not a burden but a joy, by the help of God's Spirit! In the next lesson we will more about Christ's law, the 'law of love'.

Lesson Fifteen

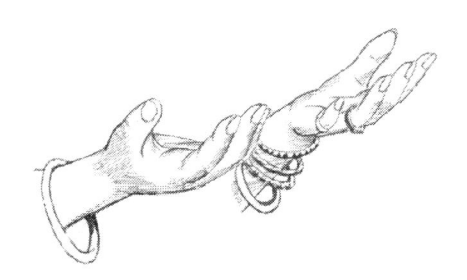

Ask God to guide you on the straight path, using this prayer of king David:

"Teach me your way, Lord; lead me in a straight path" (Psalm 27:11)

LESSON 15 PRACTICAL TASK

Getting angry is a very common sin. It is hard to control our angry words, but we can do it because God's Spirit *"gives us power, love, and self-discipline'* (2 Timothy 1:7).
- Ask God to help you not to say angry words this week;
- Each day this week, keep a count of how many times you speak in anger to another person (including your spouse and children).

LESSON 15 REVIEW

1. Compare the law of Moses with the law of Christ: *(circle the correct answers)*
   a) Which law told people the straight path but they could not follow it?
   [law of Moses / law of Christ]
   b) Which law told people the straight path <u>and</u> God's Spirit gave them strength to follow it? [law of Moses / law of Christ]

2. Who makes us willing and able to follow God's straight path? The _____ Spirit

3. What kinds of sin does Christ's law forbid? *(tick any correct answers)*
   ___ a) sinful actions (such as cheating at business)
   ___ b) sinful words (such as dirty language)
   ___ c) sinful thoughts (such as lust or pride)
   ___ d) _____ *(write your own idea)*
   ___ e) _____ (write your own idea)

4. Write the memory verse: "You are not _____
   _____ (1 Corinthians ___ : _____)

Come Follow Me

LESSON 15 ANSWERS

1. a)
2. c)
3. for discussion
4. Yes
5. You should underline: evil thoughts, sexual immorality, theft, murder, adultery, greed, malice, deceit, lewdness, envy, slander, arrogance, folly
6. Be ready to share your answer in discussion
7. Put your own name in the verse
8. spirit
9. a) No   b) Yes   c) Yes
10. Spirit
11. evil human desires, the will of God
12. b)
13. a) Yes   b) Yes
14. No
15. you should tick all these answers
16. 'Yes' for b), c), e), g) [according to 1 Peter 1:16, 1:22, 2:1 and 3:8]
    'No' for a), d), f)   [in my opinion, but bring it to discussion]
17. for discussion
18. b)
19. for discussion
20. c)
21. memorize the verse
22. c)

Study tip: Pray for your advisor, your fellow-learners, and students of this course around the world.

Lesson 16   The Law of Love

Two young men met in the market. Both were servants, and their masters had sent them to do the shopping. They started talking about their masters. "I try hard to please my master", said the first servant, "but I never know when he will get angry. I am afraid of his punishment".

"I too try to please my master", replied the other servant. "But I do it out of love, not out of fear. You see, my father was killed in the war and my mother died of cancer. I had to beg in the streets. One day a kind man found me and brought me to his home. He has done so much for me and even lets me eat at his table. I love him because he first loved me".

"I wish I could love my master", commented the first servant.

God loved us first

1   What kind of person can love God with all his heart and soul and mind and strength?
  ___ a) A person who is afraid of God's punishment
  ___ b) A person who is not afraid, because he is sure that God has forgiven him

2   We cannot fully love someone we fear. So if we are afraid of God's punishment, how can we fully love him? But hear God's comforting word to us through his apostle John:

> "There is no fear in love. But perfect love drives out fear, because fear has to do with punishment. The one who fears is not made perfect in love. <u>We love because he first loved us</u>."   (1 John 4:18-19)

Mark the following statements 'true' or 'false':
  a) God loves us because we first loved him   [True / False]
  ___ b) We love God because he first loved us   [True / False]

3   Some people think that God only loves those who do good and love him. But in fact, God loved us before we ever loved him! *"This is love: not that we loved God, but that he loved us and sent his Son as an atoning sacrifice for our sins..."* (1 John 4:10).

<u>Above all</u>, how did God prove his love to us? *(tick only one)*
  ___ a) By sending his prophets to guide us
  ___ b) By sending his books to teach us
  ___ c) By sending his Son to die for us

4   *"So we know and rely on the love God has for us"* says the same passage (1 John 4:16). Therefore, how should we now serve him?
  ___ a) from love, because he loved us first
  ___ b) from fear, because he might send us to hell.

5   In the box in question 2, look again at the underlined words, and fill the blank spaces:
  "We _____ because _____" (1 John 4:19)

Come Follow Me

God proved His Love

6   The greatest way God proved his love was when Christ died for us. The night before Jesus Christ went to the cross, he ate his last meal with his disciples. Read what he did during it:

> "Jesus took bread, and when he had given thanks, he broke it, and gave it to his disciples, saying 'Take and eat; this is my body'. Then he took a cup, and when he had given thanks, he gave it to them, saying, 'Drink from it, all of you. This is my blood of the covenant, which is poured out for many for the forgiveness of sins' "
>
> (Matthew 26:26-28)

Which two words are underlined in the passage above? _____ and _____

7   The Lord Jesus made this meal a special ceremony for his followers. We call it 'the Lord's Supper' or 'Holy Communion'. Down through all the centuries since then, his followers have regularly taken part in this ceremony. They still do so today, in every country, and they will continue this ceremony until Christ comes again.

In this ceremony, we eat a small piece of bread to remember Christ's body, and drink from a cup of grape juice or wine to remember his blood poured out for us. Who gave us this ceremony? _____

8   On the cross, the body of our Saviour Jesus was broken for us and his blood was poured out for us, when we did nothing to deserve it!

a) What do we eat in gratitude for Jesus' broken body? _____
b) From what do we drink in gratitude for his poured out blood? _____

9   Some people think that we must do things to make God love us. For them, the most important act of worship is to do the pillars of religion, especially the ritual prayers.
    But the special act of worship which Jesus commanded is the Lord's Supper. In this ceremony, we don't do anything to earn merit. Instead we receive, with grateful hearts.

What did Jesus command his followers to do in the Lord's Supper? *(tick one)*
    ___ a) 'take'   ___ b) 'give'

10   Why do we love God? 'We love, because He first _____ _____' (1 John 4:19)
(Fill the blanks from question 5)

The Law of love

11   The Lord Jesus did not cancel the law of Moses, rather he fulfilled it. One time a legal expert asked Jesus, "Of all the commandments, which is the most important?" For Jesus' reply, read Mark 12:30-31.

Christ's law is the law of love. According to Jesus Christ,
a) What is the most important commandment? " _____ the Lord your God with all your heart and with all your soul and with all your mind and with all your strength."
b) What is the second most important commandment? " _____ your neighbour as yourself."

12   What is another name for Christ's law? The law of _____ *(the same word as your answers in question 11).*

13   Write again and memorize the summary of Christ's law:

| *The first commandment*: " Love the _____ your _____ with all your _____ and with all your _____ and with all your _____ and with all your _____." *The second commandment*: " Love your _____ as _____ "   (Mark 12:30-31) |

Loving God with all our hearts

14   We love God because He first loved us. Our Lord Jesus gave all of himself for us. So we give all of ourselves for him. This is not to earn anything from him but simply because we love him and thank him and belong to him! He asks us:

- Will you give me your precious possessions?
- Will you give me your daily obedience?
- Will you give me your decisions?
- Will you give me your plans and ambitions?
- Will you give me your resentments against those who hurt you?

> *Stop and think. Out of the things listed above, which one do you find the hardest to give back to God? Put a circle round that thing.*
> *Now ask God to strengthen you to give that thing to him and to love him with all your heart.*

Loving our neighbours as ourselves

15   In Christ's summary of his law, what is the second commandment? *(see question 11)*
        "Love your _____ as yourself"

16   What does it mean, practically, to 'love your neighbour as yourself'? *(tick one)*
        ___ a) Putting the other person's needs above your own
        ___ b) Putting your own needs above the other person's

17   Even in our own families we must 'love our neighbours as ourselves'. This includes our parents, our parents-in-law, our husbands and wives, our children.

Come Follow Me

In which of the pictures below is Christ's follower putting the needs of their family member first? *(circle 'yes' or 'no' beneath each picture).*

"My wife is happy because she knows I care for her"

Picture A [Yes / No]

"You care for the baby because I am busy"

Picture B [Yes / No]

"Lord, help me to serve my mother-in-law even when she annoys me so much"

Picture C [Yes / No]

"I'm angry with my friend, so let's steal her books on the way home"

Picture D [Yes / No]

18   In your opinion, is the 'law of love' easy or hard to follow? _____

19   The law of love is so hard to follow that we cannot do it in our own strength! But, as we learned in lesson 15, God has given us a new heart and put a new spirit in us. *"God has poured out his love into our hearts by the Holy Spirit, whom he has given us".* (Romans 5:5)

How it is possible for us to love our neighbours as ourselves? *(tick one)*
  ___ a) because those people are kind to us, so we love them in return
  ___ b) because God has poured his love into our hearts by the Holy Spirit
  ___ c) because we try very hard to love them by our own efforts

20   We should love not only those who belong to our own family, neighbourhood or clan. God's Word commands us to love others also.

a) Read 1 Peter 2:17   Whom does this verse command us to love?
'the _____ of _____'

b) Read 1 Peter 3:8   Whom does this verse tell us to love? 'one _____'

112

Lesson Sixteen

21   As we learned in lesson 7, we are spiritual brothers and sisters with all of Christ's followers. We must love them.

Read 1 Peter 4:8-9 According to verse 8, how should we love? 'love each other _____'

22   We are told to love one another deeply. We should show this in practical ways. Here is a true account.

> One time in Indonesia three ladies were sentenced to prison because of their Christian witness. Their Christian brothers and sisters did not neglect them. Instead, one person drove 60 kilometres every day by motorbike to meet them in prison and take care of their needs. Every week the whole group of believers travelled to the prison to share in worship with them.

Think about any brother or sister in Christ you know, who is in need at this time. Write here one practical thing you can do to 'love that person as yourself'. _____

Be ready to share your idea in discussion.

23   Another practical way to show love is given in 1 Peter 4:9. What way is this? 'Offer _____ to one another without grumbling'.

24   Therefore, if a Christian brother or sister visits us from a different city, or if the local group of believers wants to meet in our home, can we 'offer hospitality without grumbling'? Should we be like Farida or like Asghar below? _____

Farida: "We are glad to serve these guests with whatever we have, for they are our brothers and sisters in Christ"

Asghar: "What a burden! These guests create extra trouble for us, and it costs so much to feed them!"

Come Follow Me

25   Finally, loving our 'neighbour' is not limited just to our relatives, or even to our brothers and sisters in Christ. The Lord Jesus taught,

> "You have heard that it was said, 'Love your neighbour and hate your enemy.' But I tell you, love your enemies and pray for those who persecute you"
> (Matthew 5:43-44)

Whom does Christ expect us to love? *(tick one)*
   ___ a) just our friends and neighbours
   ___ b) our friends, our neighbours and even our enemies

> Is it possible for us to love our enemies? Is it practical? Let's talk about this in the discussion time.

LESSON 16 PRACTICAL TASK

In question 22 you wrote one practical thing you can do to help a needy brother or sister in Christ. Do that thing this week. (Or if that's not possible at this time, find another way to show love to a fellow-believer this week).

LESSON 16 REVIEW

1   Christ's summary of his law contains two commands and we should obey them both. What are they?

> **The first commandment**: "Love the _____ your _____ with all your _____ and with all your _____ and with all your _____ and with all your _____."
> **The second commandment**: "Love your _____ as _____"   (Mark 12:30-31)

2   What is another name for Christ's law? The law of _____ *(question 12)*

3   Mark the following statements 'true' or 'false':
   ___ a) God loves us because we first loved him   [True / False]
   ___ b) We love God because he first loved us   [True / False]

LESSON 16 ANSWERS

1. b)
2. b)
3. c) (Even more than books or prophets, God proved his love by sending his Son)
4. a)
5. love, he first loved us
6. bread, cup
7. Jesus Christ
8. a) bread   b) cup
9. a)
10. loved us
11. a) love   b) love
12. love
13. Lord, God, heart, soul, mind, strength, neighbour, yourself
14. talk with God about this
15. neighbour
16. a)
17. Picture A: Yes   Picture B: No   Picture C: Yes   Picture D: No
18. in my opinion, it is hard!
19. b)
20. a) family, believers   b) another
21. deeply
22. personal answer, for discussion
23. read the verse
24. Farida
25. b)

Study tip: Each verse you memorize is like another coin in your treasure box.

Lesson 17   <u>Fasting and Giving</u>

> Let's recall what we have learned about Christ's law which is the 'law of love':
> - God commands us to walk in his straight path;
> - In our own strength we cannot manage this, but the Holy Spirit makes us <u>willing</u> and <u>able</u> to obey God;
> - The summary of Christ's law is to love God with all our heart and to love our neighbour as ourselves;
> - We love because he first loved us!
>
> Today we learn how God guides us on the straight path, using fasting and giving as examples.

How does God guide us on the Straight Path?

1   The Bible gives us clear guidelines for how to follow God's straight path. It tells us the character and behaviour we should have. But it does not give us many detailed regulations, especially in the New Testament. There is a good reason for this. Look at these pictures:

In Western countries, a shepherd leaves his sheep alone in a field. He builds a fence round the field to stop the sheep escaping.	By contrast, in the East, there is no need for a fence. The shepherd himself stays close to the sheep and guides them personally.
Picture 1	*Picture 2*

a) In picture 1, what stops the sheep escaping? _____
b) In picture 2, who guides the sheep personally? _____

2   This example helps us understand how Christ's rule works in our lives.

a) Which picture, 1. or 2., is like humans who need detailed laws to stop them escaping into sin? ___
b) Which picture, 1. or 2., is like Christ's followers who willingly follow wherever he leads them? ___

3   Sheep without a shepherd need a fence. People without God need detailed laws.   But we are God's chosen people! Jesus Christ is our 'good shepherd'. *"The sheep listen to his voice. He calls his own sheep by name and leads them out... He goes on ahead of them, and his sheep follow him because they know his voice".* (John 10:3-4)

Therefore, how can we best find God's guidance for our lives?
    ___ a) by keeping close to Jesus our shepherd and obeying his voice
    ___ b) by having a detailed list of regulations to obey

4   Although we cannot see Jesus our shepherd physically, he is with us by his Spirit. He guides us on the straight path, by his written Word and by his Spirit speaking quietly within us. So we should listen carefully!
As we learned in lesson 4, who has the Holy Spirit? *(tick one)*
    ___ a) every human
    ___ b) everyone who has invited Christ into his life
    ___ c) only a few special Christians

5   What two ways have we learned, by which God guides us on the straight path? *(tick two)*
    ___ a) through his Word, the Bible
    ___ b) through his Spirit within us
    ___ c) through a complete list of what is 'compulsory' or 'forbidden'

Of course, Christ's followers still need <u>some</u> written rules – for instance, murder and adultery are forbidden. But the New Testament contains fewer detailed rules than you had in your previous religion. So you need to listen to Christ's voice through his Spirit within you. Let's see how this works with the examples of fasting and giving.

Fasting

6   Without detailed regulations, how can perform our religious duties correctly? Christ's follower Parveen is worried about this in relation to fasting (*sawm* or *roza*):

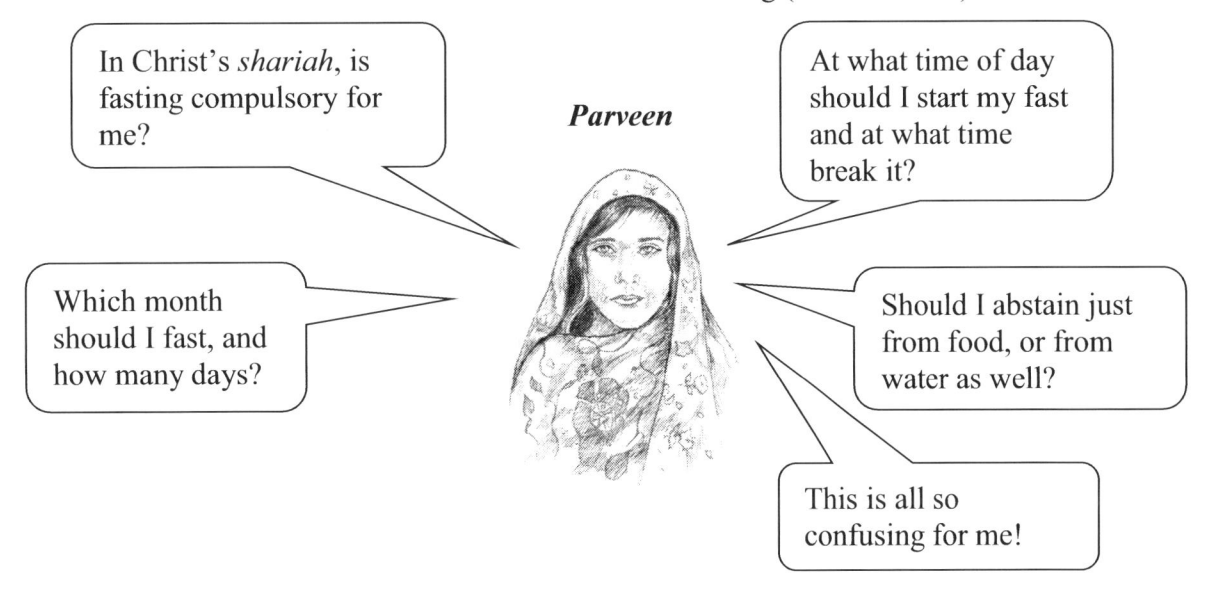

In Christ's *shariah*, is fasting compulsory for me?

At what time of day should I start my fast and at what time break it?

Parveen

Which month should I fast, and how many days?

Should I abstain just from food, or from water as well?

This is all so confusing for me!

Come Follow Me

According to what we learned above, in what two main ways will God guide Parveen about fasting? *(tick two)*
      ___ a) through a detailed list of regulations
      ___ b) through his Word, the Bible
      ___ c) through his Spirit within her

7   So, concerning fasting:
- *God's Word* gives Parveen <u>general</u> guidelines about how and why to fast; and
- *God's Spirit* gives Parveen <u>specific</u> guidance, telling her when to fast.

a) What gives general guidelines to Christ's followers?   God's _____
b) Who shows us how to apply this in specific ways?   God's _____

8   The Holy Bible gives Parveen general guidelines about 'why' to fast and 'how' to fast.

Why should we fast?
Parveen reads in God's Word that his chosen people fasted at times of danger or repentance or mourning. Fasting was their expression of earnest prayer. It showed God that they were serious. They desperately needed his help. They cried out to their Lord with their voices and also with their stomachs!

According to the general guidelines in God's Word, why should we fast? *(tick one)*
      ___ a) as an expression of earnest prayer
      ___ b) to gain religious merit

How should we fast?
9   Parveen reads in the Bible that:
- Sometimes God's people fasted just for one day, sometimes for many days;
- Sometimes they fasted just from food and sometimes from water also;
- Sometimes they fasted continuously and sometimes they stopped in the evening.

From this, Parveen realizes that the Holy Bible does not give detailed regulations on these matters. Instead what does God's Word give us? general _____

10   In teaching us 'how' to fast, God is more concerned about our inner motive than our outer appearance. Read Matthew 6:16-18 where Jesus Christ teaches us 'how' to fast.

In this passage,
a) Which verse says that the 'hypocrites' make their faces sad to show off to everyone that they are fasting? verse ____

b) Which verse says that God our Father sees it when we fast in secret? verse ____

11   According to the general guidelines in God's Word, <u>how</u> should we fast?
          ___ a) to please other people
          ___ b) to please our heavenly Father

When should we fast?

12   Parveen reads that Jesus himself was 'led by the Spirit' into a particular time of fasting (Matthew 4:1). Parveen follows Christ's pattern (*sunnah*). She too is led by the Holy Spirit. One time Parveen fasts to pray earnestly for her friend's sick child. Another time she cries out to God to grant salvation to her non-Christian family. Another time she fasts in deep repentance. Each time, by listening to the Holy Spirit's voice, she knows when to fast.

How do we know exactly <u>when</u> we should fast?
          ___ a) through detailed regulations
          ___ b) through God's Spirit guiding us

13   God's Spirit guides us not only as individuals, but also as a group. Under God's guidance our leaders may call us to fast and pray together for a specific purpose at a specific time. Also, around the world many Christians fast during the forty days before Easter. Through fasting they dedicate themselves to God and learn self-discipline.

Stop and think:
> ***Do you ask God to guide you when to fast? Or have you been lazy in fasting since becoming Christ's follower?***

14   Parveen has one more question:

> 'My family members are not yet Christ's followers. Should I fast with them in Ramadan or not?'

What do you think? Write one reason for Parveen to fast with her family, and one reason against:

For: _____

Against: _____

Be ready for discussion.

Giving

15   Khalid belongs to the same local group of believers as Parveen. His questions are similar to hers:

Khalid

- In Christ's *shariah*, must I give *zakat* (charity-tax)?
- If I give one-fortieth part to God, does the rest belong to me?
- To which kinds of people should I give? What are the rules for this?

What book gives Khalid general guidelines on this subject? _____

16   Khalid asked, "If I give one-fortieth part to God, does the rest belong to me?" The Bible gives a clear guideline to this question.

> King David generously gave gold, silver and other precious materials for building the magnificent house of God. The leaders followed his example and gave 'freely and whole-heartedly to the Lord.'
>
> Then David led them in this prayer:
>   "Lord...
>   everything in heaven and earth is yours...
>   But who am I, and who are my people,
>   that we should be able to give as generously as this?
>   Everything comes from you,
>   and we have given you only what comes from your hand...
>   And <u>all of it belongs to you</u>."   (a summary of 1 Chronicles 29:1-17)

According to king David's prayer, how much of our property belongs to God? *(tick one)*
     ___ a) one-fortieth   ___ b) one-tenth   ___ c) all of it

17   Everything we own belongs to our Creator. Naked we came into this world, and naked we will leave it. All our property belongs to God.
     Therefore let us not seek a detailed regulation on how much to give back to God. Instead, let's give 'freely and whole-heartedly' as king David did!

What two general guidelines have we learned from God's Word? *(circle the correct answers)*
     a) [All / some / none] of our property belongs to God
     b) We should give back to God [freely and whole-heartedly / as little as possible]

18   Think too about the example of our Lord Jesus. *"Though he was rich, yet for your sake he became poor"* (2 Corinthians 8:9). He gave up everything for us, even his life. Therefore how much should we be willing to give for him? *(tick one)*
     ___ a) everything   ___ b) nothing   ___ c) a little

Lesson Seventeen

19   Christ sets no limit on our giving. So should we give as little as possible? Not at all! On the contrary, we should give as much as possible! God's Word continues,

> "Each of you should give what you have decided in your heart to give, not reluctantly or under compulsion, for God loves a cheerful giver"   (2 Corinthians 9:7)

According to this verse, should we give reluctantly or cheerfully? _____

20   Christ's followers give cheerfully. They consider this a joy, not a burden. It is not a compulsory tax, like *zakat*. It is their voluntary gift. They give because of their love for God and their love for people in need.

What is another name for Christ's law? The law of _____

21   The verse in question 20 says *"each man should give what he has decided in his heart to give"*. In my own opinion the New Testament does not specify a fixed amount for how much we should give.

However, this is not an excuse to give as little as possible! In fact, many Christians give at least one-tenth of their income. This brings much blessing to them personally and also to God's work. It is a good principle to follow where possible.

Under the 'law of love', we want to love God with all our heart, soul, mind and strength. We are so grateful for all he has done for us! Therefore, as Christ's followers will we try to give less money than we previously gave under our old *shariah*, or more? [less / more]

22   Khalid still wants to know exactly how much he should give. Who will give him this specific guidance? *(tick one)*
      ___ a) God's Word the Bible   ___ b) the Holy Spirit within him

23   So Khalid talks to God about this.

> "O God,
> Thank you for providing for my family's needs.
> All my property belongs to you.
> Please give me specific guidance, by your Spirit, on how much I should give back to you each month.   Amen"

> ➤ *Now speak to God yourself, using the same words as Khalid.*

24   Guided by God's Spirit, Khalid decides how much he will give each month. Now he must be self-disciplined to set aside this money. In your opinion, what is the best time for Khalid to set aside this portion from his income?
      ___ a) On the first day of each month as soon as he receives his salary
      ___ b) On the last day of the month, if there is anything left over from his expenses

Come Follow Me

25   In Khalid's local fellowship are other believers who have decided to set aside money every month as their gift for God's work. So they agree to put all their gifts together in one box. They will not spend this money on their own needs. Rather, through these gifts they will show their love for God and their love for needy people. So together they seek the Holy Spirit's specific guidance on where to use the money.

If you were a member of that group, for what purposes would you suggest the money should be used? Note three ideas and be ready for discussion:

    1. _____
    2. _____
    3. _____

The Law of Love

26   Khalid gives generously because he loves God and he loves his neighbour. Parveen fasts for the same two reasons. Christ's law is the law of love! When we fully love God and love other people, we do not need many detailed regulations!

Write again the summary of Christ's law which you memorized in lesson 16.

The first commandment:
"_____ the Lord your God with all your _____
_____ "

The second commandment: "_____ your neighbour as _____ "
                                                                                                 (Mark ___ : _____)

LESSON 17 PRACTICAL TASK

If you control your own income, decide how much of it you will set aside each month to give back to God. If you don't have your own income, decide what other ways you can give generously, because of your love for God and for others.

LESSON 17 REVIEW

1   In what two main ways does God guide us on the straight path?
    a) God's _____ gives us general guidelines
    b) God's _____ gives us specific guidance

2   Why did God's people in the Bible fast? As an expression of earnest _____

3   a) How much of our property belongs to God? _____
    b) How much should we give back to him: as much as possible or as little as possible? _____

4   a) Why do we fast and why do we give generously? *(see point 14)*
    Because of our love for _____ and our love for other _____
    b) What is another name for Christ's law? The law of _____

LESSON 17 ANSWERS

1. a) the fence   b) the shepherd
2. a) 1.   b) 2.
3. a)
4. b)
5. a), b)
6. b), c)
7. a) Word   b) Spirit
8. b)
9. guidelines
10. read the passage yourself
11. b)
12. b)
13. your personal response
14. for discussion
15. God's Word / the Bible
16. c)
17. a) All   b) freely and whole-heartedly
18. a)
19. cheerfully
20. love
21. for discussion
22. b)
23. your personal response
24. in my opinion a) is better
25. for discussion
26. if you can't remember, see lesson 16 question 11

Study tip: If you find a mistake in this course, please let us know. It will help future learners.

Lesson 18 Fate and Magic

The following true account is from North Africa, where one time a group of Christ's followers faced a problem:

> "Whenever it was time for Christian worship, Ahmad felt a strong stomach ache. He also felt that something like a black wall was in front of him, preventing him from praising Jesus. Fatima wanted to pray and read the Bible, but instead words of curses filled her mind. And at nights, Sabina felt attacked by strong fear of death and horrible nightmares."

What could be holding these believers back from making spiritual progress? We will find out in today's lesson.

In fact all these believers had previously been involved in magic practices, such as visiting shrines, wearing amulets and living in homes which were under a curse.

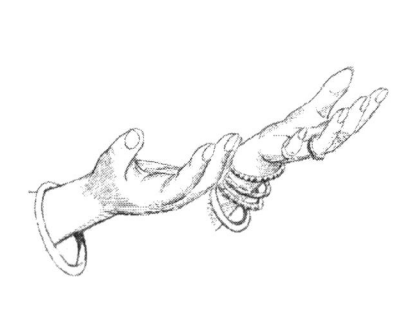

> Before studying this subject today, let's pray:
>
> *"Almighty God,*
> *You have authority over all spiritual forces which try to harm us. We trust in your protection as we study today's lesson. In the mighty name of Jesus Christ, Amen"*

1   Do you think there is any harm in magic and practices like wearing amulets or visiting shrines? Give your own opinion:

[Yes / No / I'm not sure] *(circle one)*

2   But more than our own opinion, we need to know what God's Word teaches about fate and magic. Today we will learn three truths. Here is the first one:

A) God guides our lives, not Fate
Many people have a false idea about Almighty God. They think he is too far away to be interested in their daily lives!   Their idea of God is like this:

Lesson Eighteen

People's False Idea:
```
ALMIGHTY GOD
'too far away to care'
        ↕
    WE HUMANS
```

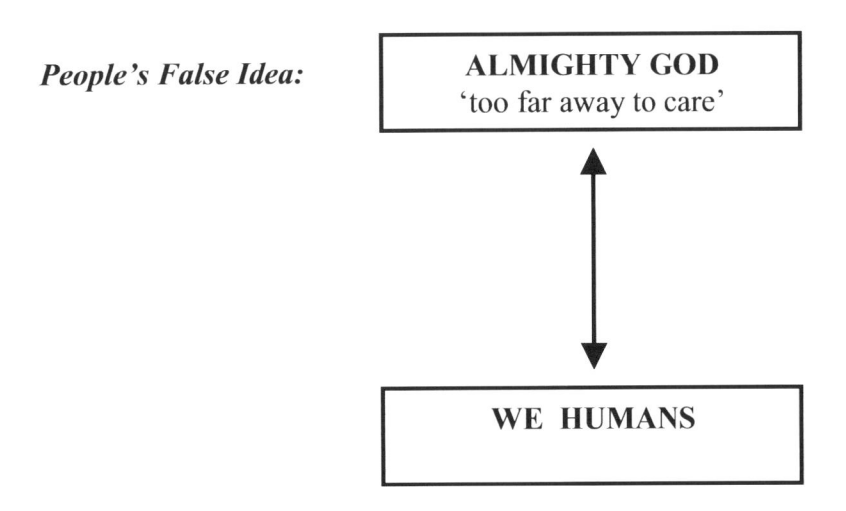

What idea of God do these people have? *(tick one)*
   ___ a) they think God is far away and does not care about their lives
   ___ b) they think God comes close and cares about their problems

3   Such people suppose that other 'spiritual powers' are closer than God himself. They think these other powers influence their daily lives for good or evil. Within each oval space below, write one of the following 'powers' which people believe in:
   angels – evil eye – fate – *jinn* – evil spirits

People's False Idea:
```
ALMIGHTY GOD
'too far away to care'
        ↓
'SPIRITUAL    ( ) ( ) ( ) ( ) ( )
 POWERS':
        ↓
    WE HUMANS
```

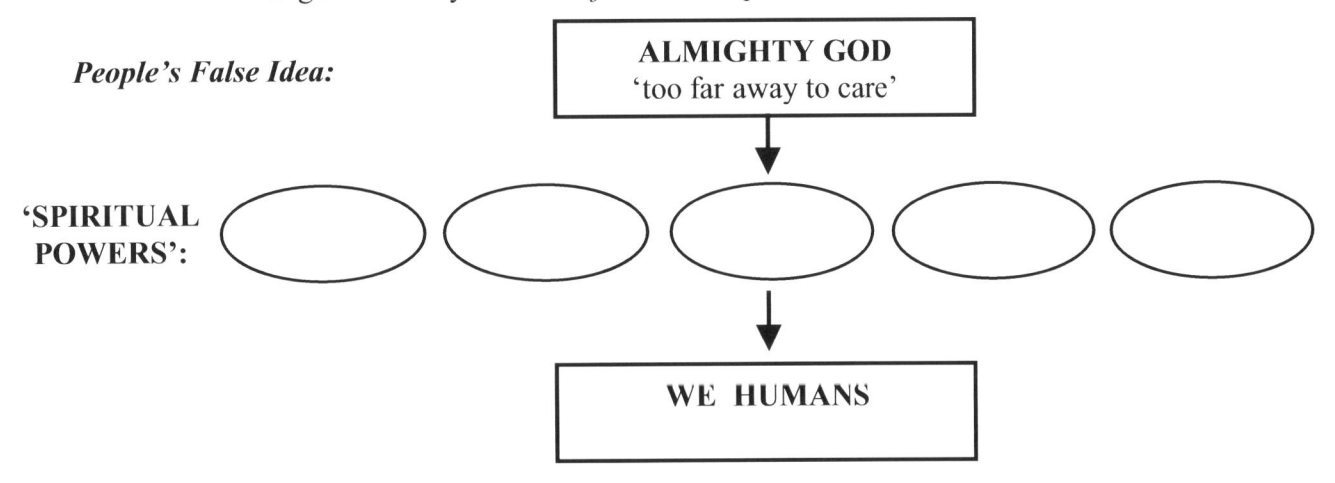

4   These people feel their lives are controlled by 'fate'. They think that nothing can change whatever is 'written' for them. Maybe you believe in fate too?

But how can we best find out what God is <u>really</u> like?
   ___ a) from God's Word the Bible   ___ b) from people's opinions

5   In contrast to what these people think, Almighty God really does care about us! In the <u>Old Testament</u> he did not remain far away, but came close to his people. He spoke personally with them on different occasions. He listened to their prayers. King David, going through a tough time in his life, found that

> "The Lord is close to the brokenhearted and saves those who are crushed in spirit"
> (Psalm 34:18)

According to these Old Testament examples, what is God really like? *(tick one)*
   ___ a) God is too far away to care about our daily lives
   ___ b) God comes close to us and cares about our problems

Come Follow Me

6   Suppose your friend's young son has just died. You go to pay condolences. You are thinking:

What comforting words can I give my friend in his grief?

1. You could say to your friend,
"Don't mourn. This was God's will. It was fate and nothing can be done about it"

2. Or you could say, in the words of Psalm 34,
"The Lord is close to the broken-hearted and saves those who are crushed in spirit"

In your opinion,
    a) Which answer, 1. or 2., gives deeper comfort? _____
    b) Which answer shows what God is really like? _____

7   In the <u>New Testament</u>, God Almighty came even closer to share in our lives. He came as a human being, Jesus Christ! Jesus came down to our level. So he cares for us and shares our sorrows.

What God is really like

ALMIGHTY GOD
'he really cares for us'

'SPIRITUAL POWERS':

JESUS CHRIST

WE HUMANS

Our Lord Jesus himself experienced sorrow and suffering. So, does he care about our problems? _____

8   The Lord really does care! Therefore when we have problems in life, we should not speak of heartless fate. Nor should we turn for help to other spiritual powers. Instead let us come close to God:

"Cast all your anxiety on him because he cares for you" (1 Peter 5:7)

Write here this precious verse, and memorize it now:
"Cast _____ (__ Peter ___ : ___)

9   *"I know the plans I have for you" declares the Lord, "plans to prosper you and not to harm you, plans to give you hope and a future"* (Jeremiah 29:11). Fate is impersonal, it has no heart. But God our Father is personal! And his heart beats for us!

Who guides the lives of God's chosen people? *(tick one)*
    ___ a) Fate   ___ b) God our Father

B) God detests Magic and Idolatry

10   Many men and women seek refuge in magical practices. They do this to seek help for their problems. They might tie an amulet to seek protection from the evil eye, or go to a shrine in the hope of healing, or sacrifice an animal (as *sadaqa*). Others think palm-reading will tell their future. Some even use black magic to gain revenge on their enemies.

Do people in your neighbourhood do such practices? For what purposes? (*Write your own opinion*) _____
_____
_____

11   Some people think there is no harm in using magic to contact spiritual powers. But let's learn what God says about this, in his Word.

Read Deuteronomy 18:10-12 . (Deuteronomy is the fifth book in the Bible. Find the page number from the 'List of Contents').

From this passage, answer the following questions:

a) Which verse forbids 'divination'?   Verse ___
    (this means trying to predict the future, e.g. through palm-reading, horoscopes, etc.)
b) Which verse forbids 'sorcery' and 'witchcraft'?   Verse ___
    (this includes all kinds of magic, such as 'casting spells' in verse 11.)
c) Which verse forbids interpreting 'omens'?   Verse ___
    (for instance, looking for patterns of tea-leaves in a cup.)
d) Which verse forbids a 'medium or spiritist or one who consults the dead'?   Verse ___
    (e.g. visiting shrines to contact the spirits of dead saints.)

12   Deuteronomy chapter 18 forbids all these magical practices: "Anyone who does these things is _____ to the Lord" *(see verse 12 and fill the blank space)*

13   Ezekiel 13:18 says, *"Woe to the women who sew magic charms on all their wrists"*.

What practice is condemned here? *(tick one)*
    ___ a) visiting shrines   ___ b) amulets   ___ c) palm-reading

14   Read 1 Peter 4:3. What is the last sin mentioned in this list? 'detestable _____'

15   God detests idolatry. One kind of idolatry is to blindly follow 'holy men' instead of following God directly, and God detests it. An idol is any created thing we worship instead of the Creator Himself. Anything we <u>trust in</u> or <u>follow</u> or <u>obey</u> more than him is *shirk* (associating something with God)!

If we trust in amulets, or follow horoscopes, or blindly obey our 'holy man', is this a kind of idolatry?
                                                            [Yes / No]

16   It is easy to trust God when he answers our prayers as we wish. But it is harder if we don't receive the answers we want. What advice would you give to this disappointed lady who is Christ's follower?

> I have prayed for many years for God to give me a child. But I am still childless! Therefore I will go to the 'holy man', maybe his prayers will be answered because he is closer to God than me.

Write your advice to this lady, and be ready for discussion _____

_____

_____

17   God detests all kinds of magic because they are idolatry. Why would we trust in any of these things instead of trusting in our Saviour? After drinking the fresh water of salvation from the spring of life, why would we turn back to stale pond-water?

Until now, we have learned two truths about fate and magic. Fill the gaps:
    a) God guides our lives, not _____ *(questions 2-9)*
    b) God _____ magic and idolatry *(question 10-17)*

Here is today's third truth:

C) The Lord Jesus rules over all Spiritual Powers

18   All around the world people are afraid of evil spirits. But when the Lord Jesus came to this earth he never feared evil spirits. Rather, they were afraid of him!

> A man... who was possessed by an impure spirit cried out, 'What do you want with us, Jesus of Nazareth? Have you come to destroy us? I know who you are – the Holy One of God!' 'Be quiet!' said Jesus sternly. 'Come out of him!' The impure spirit shook the man violently and came out of him with a shriek.
>
> The people were all so amazed that they asked each other, 'What is this? ... He even gives orders to impure spirits and they obey him"   (Mark 1:23-27)

Did this unclean spirit obey or disobey Christ's command? _____

19   The Lord Jesus rules over all spiritual powers. He has gone up to heaven, and 1 Peter 3:22 mentions three powers which are now 'in submission to him'. Write these three in the three oval spaces on this diagram.

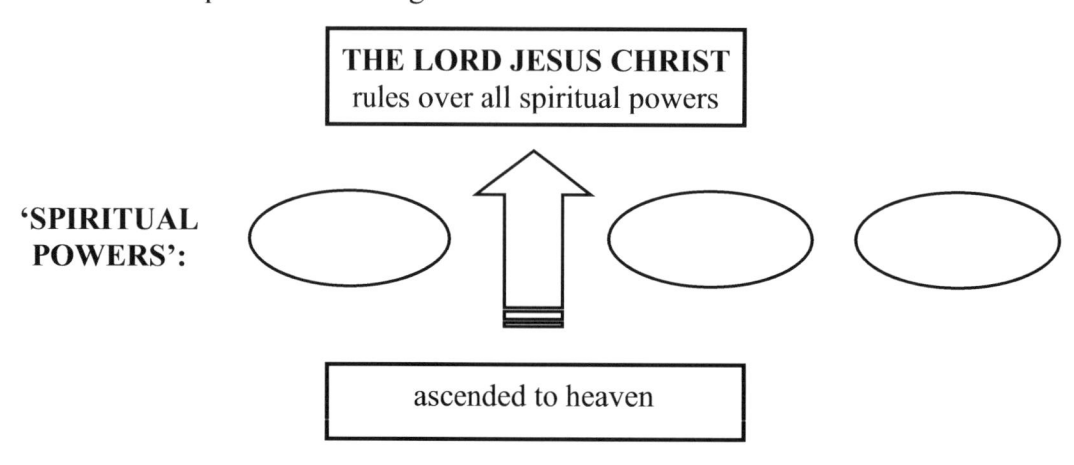

THE LORD JESUS CHRIST
rules over all spiritual powers

'SPIRITUAL POWERS':   ( )   ( )   ( )

ascended to heaven

Lesson Eighteen

20   The Lord Jesus also gave his followers *"authority to drive out impure spirits"* (Matthew 10:1).

a) Who is more powerful: impure spirits, or us in our own strength? _____

b) Who is more powerful: impure spirits, or us in Christ? _____

21   When evil spirits attack us or our loved ones, we command them to go – in the mighty name of Jesus Christ and by the power of his Spirit. And they will obey us!

In whose mighty name do we command evil spirits to leave? _____

[Please remember that this is a tough ministry, and sometimes the spirits resist the command for a long time. Also, it is sometimes difficult to tell the difference between spirit possession and mental illness. For these reasons it is not wise to do battle against evil spirits on your own. Always ask the advice of a more experienced Christian.]

Can we serve Two Masters?

22   A person who tries to follow Christ and at the same time follows a 'holy man', is like someone trying to ride two horses at the same time. Neither will Satan be pleased with him, nor will Christ!

So, if you have chosen to follow Christ, is it wise or right to keep visiting shrines?
    [Yes/No]

23   Someone said,

"A man dreamt he had a house with five rooms. He gave one room to Jesus. But a thief came and stole some things. The man asked Jesus, 'Why did you not stop him?' Jesus replied, 'Because the house is not mine'. So the man gave Jesus four rooms and kept back only one.

But the thief came again. The man was very disappointed and asked Jesus the same question as before. Jesus replied, 'Only if you give me the whole house can I control who comes in and who doesn't'.

Then in the dream the man gave all five rooms to Jesus. And the thief never came back."

What do you think this dream means? *(note your ideas and be ready for discussion)*
_____
_____

24   When we turn to Christ, we should renounce and turn away from all kinds of magic. This is what new believers did in a town called Ephesus: *"A number who had practised sorcery brought their scrolls together and burned them publicly... In this way the word of the Lord spread widely and grew in power"* (Acts 19:19-20).

These scrolls contained their magic spells, and were worth a lot of money. But what did these new believers do? *(tick one)*

        ___ a) they continued to do magic as well as follow Christ
        ___ b) they sold their magic scrolls and gave the money to the poor
        ___ c) they renounced magic and publicly burnt the scrolls

Come Follow Me

> This week's practical task will help you recognize if there are any magical practices you should renounce in your life.
>
> And do you remember the North African believers at the beginning of our lesson? When they renounced their previous magical practices the spiritual attacks ceased!

LESSON 18 PRACTICAL TASK

Think back over your life:

- Have you ever sought help from shrines or holy men or witches? Have you used verses of a holy book for amulets or drinking with water? Have you ever tried to contact the spirits of the dead?
- Do you think your parents or ancestors were active in witchcraft or magic?
- So far as you know, has anyone ever placed a curse on you?
- Are there any objects presently in your home which you think should be destroyed?
- Have you repeatedly experienced a strong fear of death, or the presence of evil in any particular place in your home?
- Do you ever experience physical pains or mental blockages when worshipping God in the name of Jesus?

Not everyone has been affected by these harmful influences. But if you think you have, then ask an experienced follower of Christ to guide you in renouncing them.

LESSON 18 REVIEW

1. What three truths about fate and magic have we learned in this lesson?
   (see question 17)
   a) God guides our lives, not _____
   b) God _____ magic and idolatry
   c) The Lord Jesus rules over all spiritual _____

2. Write this week's memory verse: *(see question 8)*
   "Cast _____ because he _____" (1 Peter ___ : ___)

LESSON 18 ANSWERS

1. your own opinion (maybe you will change it during this lesson)
2. a)
3. write the five words in the five spaces
4. a)
5. b)
6. in my opinion, *2.* is a better answer for both a) and b)
7. Yes he does care
8. memorize the verse
9. b)
10. for discussion
11. read the verses and find the answers yourself
12. detestable
13. b)
14. idolatry
15. Yes
16. for discussion
17. a) fate   b) detests
18. obey
19. write the words 'angels', 'authorities', 'powers'
20. a) impure spirits   b) us in Christ
21. Jesus Christ
22. No
23. for discussion
24. c)

Study tip: Is this course bringing positive change in your life? Can your family members see it?

Lesson 19   Serving one another

One time Jesus Christ was having a meal with his twelve disciples. They were arguing among themselves about *"which one of us is the greatest?"*

Jesus their master rebuked them: *"The greatest among you should be like the youngest, and the one who rules like the one who serves. For who is greater, the one who is at the table or the one who serves? Is it not the one who is at the table? But I am among you as one who serves."* (Luke 22:26-27)

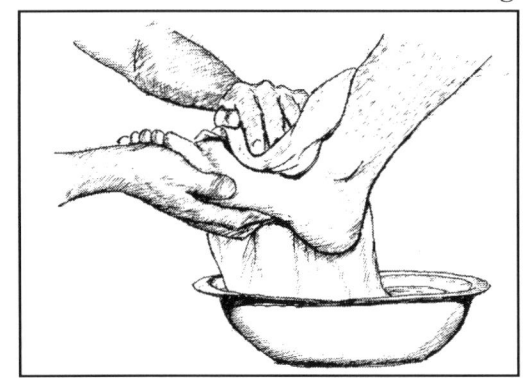

Then Jesus proved his point in an astonishing way. He got up from the table and took the place of a slave. He took off his outer clothes and tied a towel round his waist and poured water into a basin and started to wash the feet of his disciples!

What do you think about this surprising act? Would Jesus lose his follower's respect by serving them in this way? Or is it possible to serve and lead at the same time? Today we will learn how to serve one another, according to Jesus' example.

Serving One Another

1   After washing his disciples' feet, Jesus said to them:

"You call me 'Teacher' and 'Lord', and rightly so, for that is what I am. Now that I, your Lord and Teacher, have washed your feet, you also should wash one another's feet. I have set you an example that you should do as I have done for you".   (John 13:13-15)

a) In this passage, two titles show Jesus' authority over his disciples. What are these titles?
'Teacher' and '_____'
b) By washing the disciples' feet, did Jesus lose his authority over them? [Yes / No]

2   Jesus Christ did not lose his disciples' respect by serving them. In fact, soon afterwards he served them by sacrificing his life for them! As a result, they respected and loved him even more.

From the last sentence in the box, fill the blank spaces:
"I have set you an example that _____"

3   Jesus said "You should do as I have done for you". Jesus is our Teacher and our Lord. According to his example, what should we do? *(tick one)*
   ___ a) serve one another
   ___ b) rule over one another
   ___ c) compete with one another

4   Afterwards Simon Peter followed the example of his Teacher. Let's learn from 1 Peter chapters 4 and 5, where the apostle Peter teaches us how to serve one another.

Gifts for Service (1 Peter 4)

Read 1 Peter 4:10-11 and fill the blank:
"Each of you should use whatever _____ you have received to serve others" (1 Peter 4:10)

5   This is our memory verse for this lesson. Write it again and memorize it:

"Each of you _____ others" (1 Peter ___:___)

> From 1 Peter 4:10-11, we learn three things about these gifts for service:
> A. Different people have different gifts
> B. Each of us has a gift
> C. We should use our gifts humbly

A) Different People have different gifts

6   1 Peter 4:10 speaks of 'God's grace in its various forms'. God gives different gifts to different people. Some gifts are natural abilities which develop from our birth. Others are supernatural abilities we receive after our 'new birth'.

Who gives all these gifts? _____

7   All these abilities come from our generous God, through his Spirit. We cannot earn them. They are God's free gifts for his chosen people.

Write 'True' or 'False' by the following statements:
    a) Different people have different gifts   _____
    b) We earn God's gifts by doing good   _____

8   Think about a beautiful Persian carpet. If all the threads in a carpet were the same colour, how boring that would be! Instead, the weaver combines threads of many different colours into a lovely design.

In the same way, God weaves us together to be His beautiful chosen people! Does He give us all the same gifts, or different gifts? _____

9   Because we all have different gifts, we need each other. It is like a body with many parts. If we had many eyes in our face but no ears, how useless that would be! In Christ's community different people have different gifts, so we need each other.

Did you hear the story about two men? One was blind and the other crippled. They both needed to get to the city centre. But the blind man couldn't see which way to go and the crippled man couldn't walk. So how could they reach there?

Well, the blind man told the cripple to get on his back, and be his 'eyes' for him and he would be the 'feet' for the cripple. By helping each other, they both reached their destination. They served each other and trusted each other.

Think about this true story. In what ways does it apply to us in our local group of believers?

Note your ideas and be ready for discussion. _____
_____
_____

B) Each of us has a Gift

10 Here again is the verse we memorized:
"Each of you should use whatever gift you have received to serve others".
(1 Peter 4:10)

a) Does each of Christ's followers have a gift from God? [Yes / No]
b) Therefore do you yourself have a gift to use in Christ's service? [Yes / No]

11 It doesn't matter if you are old or young, male or female, educated or not! God has given each of us a gift for serving others.

Some people think they have no useful gift for service. In a local group of believers, two ladies are discussing this:

> I am just a housewife, busy with my children. I am not gifted to serve in the church!

> That's not true, dear Fayzia. You are very good at encouraging people. You notice when they are sad. You lift them up. You pray for them. God has given you the gift of encouragement, and it is very special for us!

Fayzia   *Laila*

What gift for service has God given to Fayzia? *(tick the correct answer)*
     ___ a) a gift of preaching
     ___ b) a gift of encouraging others
     ___ c) a gift of healing

12   Never think you are insignificant. Others in the church need you. God wants you to use your gift to serve his chosen people.

In every local church, how many people have gifts for service?
     ___ a) only the leaders
     ___ b) only those who are well educated
     ___ c) each person, even the shy and humble member

13   We find out our gifts by trying out different kinds of service. Then we ask ourselves:

"When I serve in this way,
- Do other believers think I am good at it?
- Do I see positive results from it?
- Do I enjoy it?"

For instance, suppose a young man Samir <u>enjoys</u> leading the singing when the believers worship together. They tell him he is <u>good at it</u>, and there are <u>positive results</u> as people's hearts are lifted in praise to God.

So then, what is Samir's gift for service? _____

14   That way is how we discover our gifts for service. But as we do so, there is a danger! We may develop a wrong attitude. We may become proud of our own gifts, or jealous of other people's gifts.

So we need to learn a third thing too:

C) We should use our Gifts Humbly

Recall our memory verse once more, and fill the blank space: *"Each of you should use whatever gift you have _____ to serve others"*. (1 Peter 4:10)

15   The verse reminds us that we 'receive' gifts. We cannot earn them and we do not deserve them! They all come from God's generous hand.

Here again is the young man Samir from question 13. He has many gifts:

I am good at leading, singing, and evangelism, and praying for the sick. I understand the Bible very well. I preach excellent sermons. I even speak in supernatural tongues. I have more gifts than anyone else in my local church. So why didn't they make me their leader?

If you were a member of that church, would you want Samir to be the leader? Write reasons for and against giving him responsibilities as leader, and be ready for discussion.

Reasons <u>for</u> Samir being leader: _____

_____

Reasons <u>against</u> Samir being leader: _____

_____

16   Proud Samir has forgotten that <u>we should use our gifts humbly</u>. They are for us to serve God and to serve others.

1 Peter 4:11 gives two examples of this. Fill the blanks from this verse:

> "If anyone _____ , they should do it as one who speaks the very words of God.
> If anyone _____ , they should do it with the strength God provides"

17   1 Peter 4:11 shows that it is a big responsibility to 'preach' God's Word. Every preacher should work hard to prepare the sermon carefully.

1 Peter 4:11 also says that we should 'serve' with God's strength. This word often refers to serving a meal. Men forget how hard women work to cook delicious meals, serve them and then clear up afterwards! But to God the person who serves in this way is just as important as the one who preaches.

For what reason do we serve? *(read the rest of verse 11 in your Bible and then tick one answer)*
   ___ a) so that we may be praised by other people
   ___ b) so that in all things God may be praised through Jesus Christ

18   From 1 Peter chapter 4, what three things have we learned about gifts for service? *Fill the blank spaces:*

   a) Different people have _____ gifts   (see question 6)
   b) _____ of us has a gift   (see question 10)
   c) We should use our gifts _____   (see question 14)

Serving as Leaders (1 Peter 5)

19   Read 1 Peter 5:1-4. To whom is the apostle Peter writing this section? "To the _____" (verse 1.)

20   In the New Testament, each local church had a group of leaders. This is better than having just one leader in each church. They can share the different responsibilities according to their different gifts.

Look at this progression:

> Jesus Christ himself is the *"Chief Shepherd"* (1 Peter 5:4)

> Jesus told the apostle Peter *"take care of my sheep"* (John 21:16)

> Peter told the church leaders, *"Be shepherds of God's flock"* (1 Peter 5:2)

Lesson Nineteen

What important task has God given to church leaders? To be _____ of His flock.

21   Jesus the Chief Shepherd shows us how to be a good shepherd. He said, *"I lay down my life for the sheep"* (John 10:15).

What are the characteristics of a good shepherd? *(tick any correct answers)*
    ___ a) He is unselfish
    ___ b) He cares more for the sheep's welfare than for his own.
    ___ c) He is lazy
    ___ d) He lets the sheep wander into danger
    ___ e) He sacrifices himself for the sheep

22   1 Peter 5:2-3 tells leaders how to be unselfish shepherds of God's flock. Fill the blanks:
    a) "not because you must, _____ because you are willing" (verse 2)
    b) "not pursuing dishonest gain, _____ eager to serve" (verse 2)
    c) "not lording it over those entrusted to you, _____ being examples to the flock" (verse 3)

23   This repeated word 'but' shows that Christian leaders should be very different from worldly leaders. Just think of the difference:
- Worldly leaders use their people for their own benefit.
- Christ-like leaders sacrifice themselves for their people's benefit.

It is not easy to lead in a serving way. But what will such leaders receive as a reward? A "_____ of glory" (see verse 4).

24   Leaders have a big responsibility to care for God's people. The people's responsibility is to encourage and submit to their leaders instead of complaining. Let us be grateful for our leaders, and respect them.

Read 1 Peter 5:5-6
What attitude should the younger people show towards the elders? "_____ yourselves"

25   Whether we are leaders or members of a church, 1 Peter 5:5 tells us *"Clothe yourselves with humility towards one another"*. Just as Jesus humbly served his disciples by washing their feet, so we serve each other humbly.

At the start of this lesson, we asked 'is it possible to serve and lead at the same time?' Most people think it is impossible. But what do you think? Note your ideas and be ready for discussion: _____
_____

> Jesus completely changed the whole system of service. He was the Master, but he did the serving. So let us forget about status and position, and serve from our hearts!

LESSON 19 PRACTICAL TASK

Ask another believer, who knows you well,
"What gifts for service do you think I have? How can I use those gifts to serve others?"

LESSON 19 REVIEW

1   From 1 Peter chapter 4, what three things have we learned about gifts for service?

   a) Different people have _____ gifts   *(questions 6-9)*
   b) _____ of us has a gift   *(questions 10-14a)*
   c) We should use our gifts _____   *(questions 14b-18)*

2   Write the memory verse: "Each _____
   _____". (1 _____ ___:___)

LESSON 19 ANSWERS

1. a) Lord b) No
2. copy from the box in question 1
3. a)
4. gift
5. memorize the verse
6. God
7. a) True b) False
8. different gifts
9. for discussion
10. a) Yes b) Yes
11. b)
12. c)
13. leading the singing
14. received
15. for discussion
16. read the verse
17. b)
18. a) different b) each c) humbly
19. elders
20. shepherds
21. a), b), e) are correct
22. a) but b) but c) but
23. crown
24. submit
25. for discussion

Study tip: What has God done in your life? How has he answered your prayers? Tell us on comefollowmecourse@gmail.com.

Lesson 20   Our Pilgrimage to Heaven

> Some people talk about five 'pillars' of faith. In the Christian faith there is really only one pillar. i.e. Jesus Christ himself. He is our rock, our foundation.
>
> However Jesus' followers do also practice the five 'pillars', in a different way from other religions. We have learned about *shahaadah* (witness) in lesson 13, *salah/namaz* (ritual prayer) in lesson 5, *sawm/roza* (fasting) in lesson 17 and *zakat* (charity-tax) in lesson 17. But what about the *hajj* (pilgrimage)? Do Christ's followers have any equivalent for that?

Our Spiritual Pilgrimage

1   In the Old Testament, the people went on pilgrimage to Jerusalem for their festivals three times a year. They sang psalms like this: *"Blessed are those whose strength is in you, whose hearts are set on pilgrimage"* (Psalm 84:5). Jerusalem was the centre of their religion and the focal point (*qibla*) of their prayers.

To which city did the people of the Old Testament go on pilgrimage? _____

2   Later Jesus Christ came. He taught that God himself is the focal point for our prayers, not any particular city on earth. Of course, if Christians wish they may visit Jerusalem to see the famous places. But it is not an important part of their faith. There is no advantage for them to pray at Jesus' tomb, for his tomb is empty and he now reigns in heaven!

What is the centre of our worship as Christ's followers?
    ___ a) Jerusalem   ___ b) God himself

3   Christ's followers are on a kind of pilgrimage. But it is not to an earthly city. Rather, our whole life on earth is a spiritual pilgrimage towards our heavenly homeland.
    Our ancestor by faith is Abraham (*Ibrahim*). He lived in tents in the land of Canaan, as a foreigner, for he was looking forward to *"a place he would later receive as his inheritance"* (Hebrews 11:8). He was on a pilgrimage to his homeland.

Where is our true homeland? *(tick one)*
    ___ a) in our country where we own a house or land
    ___ b) in Jerusalem
    ___ c) in heaven with our Lord

4   We, like Abraham, are pilgrims on our way to our homeland. At last, on the day of our death, we will reach our destination. We will meet God our Father face to face!

Stop and Think about your own pilgrimage:
- ➢ *Do you strongly desire to reach your homeland in paradise?*
- ➢ *Are you pushing straight ahead towards your destination, or are you just wandering aimlessly in circles?*

Talk with God about this, before going on to the next question.

5   For me, sometimes this journey is hard and I become anxious. At other times, the path is easy and I become too confident in my own abilities. What about you?

Read 1 Peter 5:6-7. In this passage,
a) Which verse do we need when we are too anxious, verse 6 or verse 7? _____
b) Which verse do we need when we are too proud, verse 6 or verse 7? _____
(Choose verse 6 for one answer and verse 7 for the other answer)

God's Word meets our every need. In 1 Peter chapter 5, we need verse 6 when we are proud, and verse 7 when we are anxious. In the Bible whenever you find verses to meet different needs, store them up in your heart. They will be ready to help you on the relevant occasion.

Resist the Devil

6   Also, on this spiritual pilgrimage we have an enemy, called the devil or Satan. He tries to block our path and to harm us.

Read 1 Peter 5:8-9. To what animal is the devil compared in these verses? _____

7   The lion is a dangerous animal. It prowls around by the edge of the flock, ready to attack any sheep which are:
- weak, *or*
- not alert, *or*
- separated from the flock.

It is the same with us. In what ways can Christ's followers become
- weak? _____
- not alert? _____
- separated from the flock? _____

Write one example in each space, and bring them to the discussion time.

8   In the beginning the Lord made every creature good, including the angels. One of these was the devil. But later he rebelled against God. Ever since that time he has tried to destroy God's work. He *"prowls around like a roaring lion looking for someone to devour"* (1 Peter 5:8).

What advice does 1 Peter 5:8 give us concerning this 'roaring lion'?
'Be _____ and of sober mind'

Come Follow Me

9   Satan is our enemy. We should be alert because he attacks us in different ways. Sometimes he attacks us through <u>outer difficulties</u>, and sometimes through <u>inner temptations</u>.

> After Mahboob in Pakistan became Christ's follower, he faced many difficulties. First his beloved wife Samira left him. Then Samira's brothers beat Mahboob and forced him to divorce her. Then they made him give back the money they had spent on their sister's wedding. Then they lied to the judge, and Mahboob had to pay back even more than the original amount. Then Mahboob's family condemned him for the divorce, and for not being a good follower of their religion. Everyone rejected Mahboob. He was miserable and depressed.

Who attacked Mahboob through these severe outer difficulties? Not just humans but also _____

10   Yes, Satan tries to hurt our bodies, minds or spirits. He is cruel, like a lion. But this lion is on a long chain. The devil is not free to do whatever he wants. God has put limits on his power.

> In the Old Testament, we read about a man called Job (*Ayub*). He was a wealthy man with a large family. The devil wanted to attack him, but first the devil had to get God's permission. God said 'yes', but with limits.
>
> Then Satan attacked Job with many sufferings. Job lost his wealth, his health and all his children. What a great blow! But the Lord did not let Satan step over the limit of what Job could endure. Job kept trusting God despite his losses. And in the end God used it for good.

Circle the correct answers:
a) Who attacks us to harm us?   [the devil / God]
b) Who uses it for good in our lives? [the devil / God]

11   Thankfully our Father God does not allow us to be tested beyond our limit. He knew what Job could endure, he knows what Mahboob can endure and he knows what we can endure!

1 Peter 5:9 says *"the family of believers throughout the world is undergoing the same kind of sufferings"*.

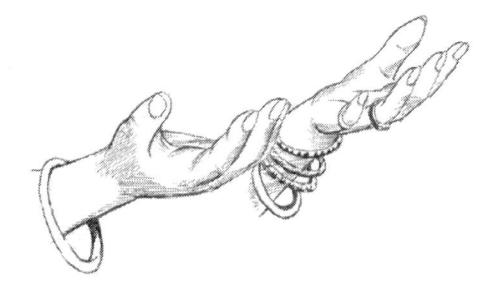

➢ ***Stop and Pray*** right now, for "the family of believers throughout the world" whom Satan is attacking through their difficult circumstances, including brother Mahboob in Pakistan.

12   The devil also attacks us by tempting us to do wrong. A lion creeps up on any animal which is unaware of danger. The devil creeps up on us and places temptations within us. We are attracted by these temptations and fall into his clutches.

The devil uses both <u>outer difficulties</u> and <u>inner temptations</u>. For each of the examples below, write 'outer difficulty' or 'inner temptation' as appropriate.

Akhtar is gripped by pornography

a) _____

Gul's husband divorces her

b) _____

Shireen plots revenge for an insult

c) _____

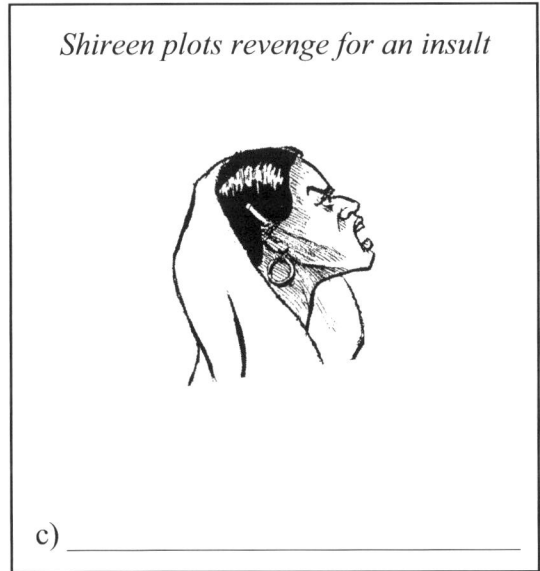

Iftikhar loses his job

d) _____

13   But we are not afraid of Satan. What command does 1 Peter 5:9 give us? '_____ him, standing _____ in the faith'.

14   Yes, we <u>can</u> resist the devil's temptations and we <u>can</u> stand firm! We ourselves don't have the strength for this, but our Lord Jesus himself lives in us and he gives us the strength. *"The one who is in you [Christ] is greater than the one who is in the world [Satan]"* (1 John 4:4). Christ defeated the devil on the cross.

Who has the strength to resist Satan? *(tick one)*

    ___ a) we ourselves   ___ b) Jesus Christ living within us

Come Follow Me

15   The <u>strength</u> to resist temptation comes from Christ. But the <u>choice</u> to resist temptation is our own.

On life's pilgrimage, many times I come to a fork in the road. At each fork, the devil tempts me to go his way, and at the same time God tests me to go his way.

Who must choose between these two ways? *(tick one)*

    ___ a) God
    ___ b) I myself
    ___ c) the devil

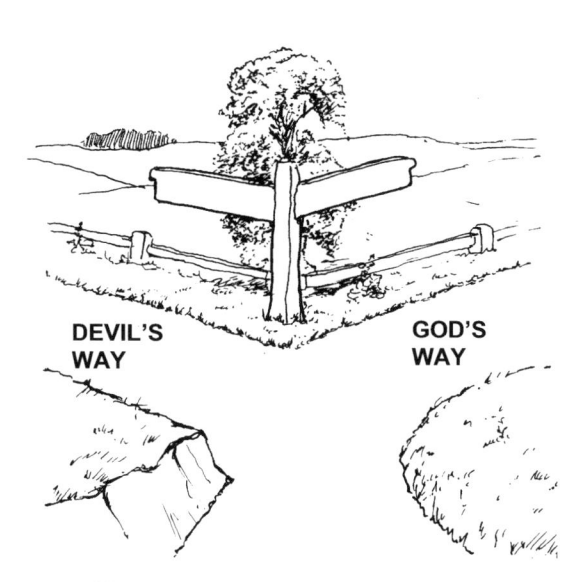

DEVIL'S WAY   **GOD'S WAY**

16   At the fork in the road, if I choose God's way I will make progress in my journey. But if I choose Satan's way, and I keep walking that way, I will stray further and further from God's path.

Whenever that happens, what must I do? I must retrace my steps and come back to God's path. I must sincerely repent and ask for God's forgiveness. He will definitely forgive me because this is his promise. Then he puts me back on his path, to continue my pilgrimage once more.

While standing firm in our faith, whom do we resist? The _____

Our Destination in Heaven

17   God will protect us on our spiritual pilgrimage until we reach our destination. In the box below, underline the words 'steadfast', 'strong', 'restore', 'firm' and 'power':

> "And the God of all grace, who called you to his eternal glory in Christ, after you have suffered a little while, will Himself restore you and make you strong, firm and steadfast. To him be the power for ever and ever. Amen."   (1 Peter 5:10-11)

18   During our pilgrimage we have 'suffered a little while'. But far more important is our 'eternal glory' in Christ! Put a circle round these two phrases in the box.

19   Do you ever doubt if you will reach your destination in heaven? Do you fear falling off a narrow bridge before reaching paradise? Read again the words in the box. Whose strength will get you safely to heaven, God's strength or your own strength? _____

20   Now memorize 1 Peter 5:10-11.

21   Our pilgrimage on this earth may be long or short, but at last we will reach our destination in heaven.

> My friend Umar was dying of cancer. He belonged to Christ, and was eagerly waiting to be with him in paradise. Before Umar died, he recited this verse to me: *"No eye has seen, no ear has heard, no mind has conceived what God has prepared for those who love him"* (1 Corinthians 2:9. 1984 version of NIV).
>
> After that I never saw Umar again. But I know he is now so happy, at home with his heavenly Father and free from pain!

Where is the destination of our pilgrimage? *(tick one)*
    ___ a) Jerusalem
    ___ b) another city
    ___ c) our homeland in heaven

22   The last two chapters in the Bible, Revelation chapters 21 and 22, give an amazing description of our heavenly city. Read both chapters when you get the chance. Here is just an excerpt:

> "Look! God's dwelling place is now among the people, and he will dwell with them. They will be his people, and God himself will be with them and be their God. He will wipe away every tear from their eyes. There will be no more death or mourning or crying or pain... No longer will there be any curse... The throne of God and of the Lamb will be in the city, and his servants will serve him. They will see his face... And they will reign for ever and ever."
> (Revelation 21:3-4, 22:3-5)

a) Read this passage aloud.
b) Now read it out again, but wherever the word 'they' comes, say 'we' instead.
(e.g. *"We will be his people, and God himself will be with us and be our God"*).

> This is the destination of God's chosen people! How much we long, with all our hearts, to complete our pilgrimage to heaven and be with our Lord forever!

LESSON 20 PRACTICAL TASK

Each day this week, take one phrase from Revelation 21 and Revelation 22 and meditate on it slowly:

Day 1: "Look! God's dwelling place is now among the people, and he will dwell with them."
Day 2: "They will be his people, and God himself will be with them and be their God."
Day 3: "He will wipe away every tear from their eyes."
Day 4: "There will be no more death or mourning or crying or pain... or any curse."
Day 5: "The throne of God and of the Lamb will be in the city, and his servants will serve him."
Day 6: "They will see his face."
Day 7: "And they will reign for ever and ever."

"God will wipe every tear from our eyes"

LESSON 20 REVIEW

1. a) To which city did the people of the Old Testament go on pilgrimage? _____
   b) Where is the destination of our spiritual pilgrimage, as Christ's followers?
   Our homeland in _____

2. When the devil tempts us,
   a) who must make the choice to resist temptation: us or Christ? _____
   b) who gives the strength to resist temptation: us or Christ? _____

3. Write again the verse you memorized *(see question 17)*:
   "And the God of all grace, _____.
   To him be _____. Amen" (1 Peter___:___)

4. Are you fully certain that when you die, God will accept you into paradise? Give your personal answer:
   ___ a) Yes, I am fully certain
   ___ b) I hope so, but I am not sure
   ___ c) I think God will torture me for some time before letting me into paradise

If you are not sure how to answer this last question, please talk privately with your advisor! This is very important.

LESSON 20 ANSWERS

1. Jerusalem
2. b)
3. c)
4. personal response
5. a) verse 7   b) verse 6
6. a lion
7. for discussion
8. alert
9. the devil or Satan
10. a) the devil   b) God
11. pray for those fellow-believers
12. a) inner temptation
    b) outer difficulty
    c) inner temptation
    d) outer difficulty
13. resist, firm
14. b)
15. b)
16. devil
17. underline the words in the box
18. circle the words in the box
19. God's strength
20. memorize the verse
21. c)
22. in a) and b) read the passage aloud

Congratulations, you have finished this course!

If you put it into practice in your daily life, it will be of lasting benefit. But if you do not put it into practice you will gradually lose the benefit.

So ask God to fill you more and more with his Spirit, to make you daily more like Jesus Christ. And whatever he tells you to do, do it!

"Now may the Lord of peace himself give you peace at all times and in every way." (2 Thessalonians 3:16)

Supplement 1: My Daily Time with God

These steps are to guide you each day in your dedicated time with God.
- *At each step, pray with your own words, or using the suggested prayers.*
- *You may stand, kneel, sit or bow down, as God's Spirit leads you.*
- *You may use these steps on your own, or together with other believers.*

Step 1:

Prepare

> **Confess your sin and ask God to cleanse you. This is like your spiritual ablution (*wudu*).**

Sample prayer:
"O Holy God, you know all my inner secrets.
Please remind me now of my wrong deeds, words or thoughts since my last prayer time [...name them here...].
I have hurt and dishonoured you in these ways.
I am sorry; please forgive me and cleanse me within.
Thank you for your promise to forgive all who truly turn back to you.
I receive your forgiveness now, through the sacrifice of Jesus the Messiah. Amen"

> **Ask God to speak with you through his Word and help you understand it.**

Sample prayer from Psalm 27:8:
"My heart says of you, 'Seek his face!' Your face, Lord, I will seek."

Step 2:

Read

> **Read a passage of the Bible**, maybe a few verses or half a chapter

> Stop at a phrase which **especially leaves its impression on you**. It may be a truth about God, a promise to assure you, an example to follow, or a command to obey.

> Do something to help you **remember this important point** God taught you today. e.g. write the verse in a notebook, or memorize it.

> **Place a book-mark** in the passage, to mark where to continue reading tomorrow with the next section.

Step 3:

Pray

➢ First, **thank God for his Word and ask his help** to put into practice what you learned today

Sample Prayer from Psalm 119:103,105
"How sweet are your words to my taste, sweeter than honey to my mouth... Your word is a lamp to my feet and a light to my path".

➢ Then **thank and praise your Father God**

Sample Prayer
"Dear heavenly Father,
You are my Creator and my Master, you are faithful and strong.
You love those who don't deserve it. You came to me in Jesus my Saviour and made me your child. Thank you!
Thank you too for meeting my needs and answering my prayers [...mention one thing God has provided for you...].
I praise and thank you my Father, Amen"

➢ Then **pray for your own needs**: your material needs, your social needs and your spiritual needs. **Also listen** to anything God wants to say to you.

➢ Then **pray for the needs of others**, perhaps using this rota:

Day	People I will pray for
Friday	My close family members
Saturday	My wider family and relatives
Sunday	Followers of Jesus in my country & worldwide
Monday	My friends who do not know Jesus
Tuesday	Any poor and sick people I know
Wednesday	The government and leaders of my country
Thursday	Christ's kingdom to spread around the world

➢ Finally you may like to pray **the Lord's Prayer**:

"Our Father in heaven,
Hallowed be your name,
Your kingdom come, your will be done, on earth as it is in heaven.
Give us this day our daily bread.
Forgive us our debts, as we have also forgiven our debtors,
And lead us not into temptation but deliver us from the evil one.
For yours is the kingdom, the power and the glory. Amen"

Now, go out into daily life, strengthened by God's Spirit to obey His Word!

Supplement 2: How to reach God

This supplement links with lesson 13. It shows some key points and a diagram to help you explain to a friend how they can reach God. Its uses 1 Peter 3:18 as the key verse.

However, if your friend is not yet ready to hear this message, you could start with stories of the prophets like Abraham, Moses and David. They point towards Jesus Christ.

God created us not just to obey him, but to love him and know him personally. We all want to reach up to Almighty God. But between us and him there is gap we cannot cross. It is called 'Our Sin'. It cuts us off from God and fill us with shame.

GOD

OUR SIN

We deserve to die and go to hell. But God Almighty loves us so much and wants to save us from that! He found a way to cross the barrier of our sin.

God's Word tells us how:

> "For Christ also suffered
> once for sins,
> the righteous for the unrighteous,
> to bring you to God"
>
> (1 Peter 3:18)

Here we see four wonderful truths:

1. <u>'For Christ also suffered'</u> He really did die on the cross, and afterwards God raised him to life again, and gave him a place of highest honour in heaven.

2. 'once for sins' This was God's plan from the beginning. In the times of Abraham and Moses, God told the people to make animal sacrifices to take away sin temporarily. But he also promised that the Messiah will come and make a perfect, permanent sacrifice 'once for sins'.

3. 'the righteous for the unrighteous' We are unrighteous and full of sin. But Jesus the Messiah was without sin, as all the books say. He, the righteous one, took our sin with its punishment and shame when he died on the cross!

4. 'to bring you to God'
Jesus Christ crossed the barrier of our sin. He himself is the 'Straight Path' to bring us to God!

He rose from the dead, he is alive today and he invites you and your whole family to follow him. He says "Come Follow Me!"

Will you accept this Straight Path which Christ made at great cost? The choice is yours:

- You can say "I don't need this Path, I can find my own way instead". But you not succeed.

    Or

- You can say "I'll think about it and maybe follow this Path another time." But don't let this prevent you from ever taking the step.

    Or

- You can step on to the Path by praying this prayer:

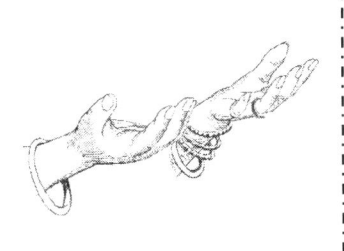

> "Dear God,
> Thank you for making a Path back to you through Jesus Christ.
> I accept him gratefully into my life.
> I turn away from my old sinful ways.
> Please forgive me and make me clean.
> Please fill me with your Holy Spirit.
> I will follow and obey you as my Master.
> Amen"

If you sincerely entrust yourself to the Lord Jesus Christ, he will keep his promise to come into your life. He will make you a new person and will join you to the community of his followers.

Feedback requested

Please answer some or all of the questions below, and send me your comments by email on comefollowmecourse@gmail.com .

This will help me improve the course in the next edition.   Thank you!   *Tim Green* (author)

---

1. a) In which country do you live?
   b) Are you a student of this course or an advisor?
   c) For how long have you been a follower of Jesus Christ?
   d) How many years of formal education have you completed?

2. Which lessons helped you most, and why?

3. Which lessons helped you least, and why?

4. What changes did God bring in your life by means of this course?

5. Which words or concepts in this course did you find hard to understand?

6. Which topics are missing in this course that are important for a new believer?

7. Do you have any other suggestions for improving this course?

Printed in Great Britain
by Amazon